JOB SKILLS AND MINORITY YOUTH

Minority youth unemployment is an enduring economic and social concern. This book evaluates two new initiatives for minority high school students that seek to cultivate marketable job skills. The first is an after-school program that provides experiences similar to apprenticeships, and the second emphasizes new approaches to improving job interview performance. The evaluation research has several distinct strengths. It involves a randomized controlled trial, uncommon in assessments of this issue and age group. Marketable job skills are assessed through a mock job interview developed for this research and administered by experienced human resource professionals. Mixed methods are utilized, with qualitative data shedding light on what actually happens inside the programs, and a developmental science approach situates the findings in terms of adolescent development. Beneficial for policymakers and practitioners as well as scholars, *Job Skills and Minority Youth* focuses on identifying the most promising tactics and addressing likely implementation issues.

Barton J. Hirsch is Professor of Human Development and Social Policy at Northwestern University, where he is also on the faculty of the Institute for Policy Research. He has published two previous books on youth programs, *A Place to Call Home: After-School Programs for Urban Youth* and *After-School Centers* and *Youth Development: Case Studies of Success and Failure* (with Nancy L. Deutsch and David L. DuBois), both of which received the Social Policy Award for Best Authored Book from the Society for Research on Adolescence.

Job Skills and Minority Youth

NEW PROGRAM DIRECTIONS

Barton J. Hirsch

Northwestern University

CAMBRIDGE
UNIVERSITY PRESS

CAMBRIDGE
UNIVERSITY PRESS

University Printing House, Cambridge CB2 8BS, United Kingdom

Cambridge University Press is part of the University of Cambridge.

It furthers the University's mission by disseminating knowledge in the pursuit of education, learning and research at the highest international levels of excellence.

www.cambridge.org
Information on this title: www.cambridge.org/9781107427709

First published 2015
First paperback edition 2016

A catalogue record for this publication is available from the British Library

Library of Congress Cataloguing in Publication data
Hirsch, Barton Jay, 1950–
Job skills and minority youth : new program directions / Barton J. Hirsch.
    pages   cm
ISBN 978-1-107-07500-9 (hardback) – ISBN 978-1-107-42770-9 (paperback)
1. Minority youth – Employment.   2. Vocational qualifications.   I. Title.
HQ796.H57   2015
331.3′46–dc23   2015022582

ISBN 978-1-107-07500-9 Hardback
ISBN 978-1-107-42770-9 Paperback

In memory of Maggie Daley

CONTENTS

vii

PREFACE

The research reported in this book began when Rachel Klein, then senior director of research and evaluation at After School Matters, came to my office to explore whether I would be interested in directing a major evaluation of the program. After School Matters, located in Chicago, had a national reputation as the flagship program for high school youth in the after-school arena. It featured apprenticeships in a wide array of areas that were designed to promote positive youth development and marketable job skills. Participants were drawn from Chicago public schools and were predominantly low-income, minority youth.

I am fairly sure that I sat up straighter, and my eyes opened wide, when Rachel told me that each of their apprenticeships recruited roughly fifty young people, though twenty-five was the limit for enrollment. I quickly suspected that a randomized controlled trial might be possible. A randomized controlled trial was considered the "gold standard" of evaluation. The youth programs that I had previously studied never had sufficient enrollment to justify using this research design. Several foundations proved quite eager to provide funding given the combination of After School Matters' intriguing program and a rigorous evaluation.

The comprehensive evaluation of After School Matters that was undertaken focused on a range of outcomes in the domains of positive youth development, marketable job skills, academics, and problem behavior. I was especially interested in that part of the evaluation that focused on marketable job skills. As part of this effort, we developed an important new assessment, a mock job interview for high school students, administered by human resource professionals, and the results bore on a major national concern: the high rate of minority youth unemployment. Moreover, our initial evaluation of After School Matters led organically to the development of a promising new intervention to improve the job interview skills of high school students in the Chicago Public Schools district (which encompasses all of Chicago). Accordingly, this book focuses on the domain of marketable job skills, or youth workforce development, in both After School Matters and the job interview training program. At the same time, I can certainly appreciate that some readers will be interested in the complete set of evaluation findings, and to have these accessible in one place, outcomes in the areas of positive youth development, academics, and problem behavior are presented in Appendix 1.

Accordingly, the book is written for those whose primary interest is in programs to increase minority youth employment, as well as those whose main interest is in positive youth development programs. I have enjoyed the challenge of writing both for those who do and those who do not have a technical background in research. Technical, methodological and statistical points are primarily placed in notes so that those who would like the details can have access to them. To keep the text as readable as possible, I have placed citations to prior publications as footnotes rather than in the main body of the text. Extensive qualitative data about the apprenticeships are presented, as well as the most important quantitative findings.

This book is a result of the efforts of many people who have contributed to and collaborated with the research team during both projects.

I am grateful to the staff of After School Matters, including David Sinski, who was Executive Director at the time of the research, and Rachel Klein, Raymond Legler, and Natasha Smith. Thanks to all the regional directors and specialists who worked hard and assisted in recruitment and planning, and to the apprenticeship instructors who generously allowed access to their programs. The evaluation benefited from the cooperation of Chicago Public Schools principals, staff, and teachers in whose schools the apprenticeships took place. Of course the study would not have been possible without the many young people who graciously participated in the research.

I thank the many human resource professionals who volunteered their time to conduct mock job interviews in the three years of data collection, as well as during the job interview training program that we later developed. I am particularly grateful to Cheryl Berrington and Wilbert Williams, whose contributions were invaluable in the design of the Northwestern Mock Job Interview. Baker & McKenzie LLP generously provided us with access to their meeting rooms for sessions with the human resource professionals.

At Northwestern, I am especially appreciative of the many contributions of my colleague Larry Hedges. Larry directed the more sophisticated statistical analyses and was an unfailing source of sound advice whenever called upon (he is also a coauthor of Appendix 1). The study could not have been completed without the help of Kathadin Cook, Megan Mekinda, Jaime Platzer, Deborah Puntenney, Christy Serrano, JulieAnn Stawicki, and Oseela Thomas, who observed apprenticeships and conducted interviews with participants and after-school instructional staff. Special thanks to JulieAnn Stawicki and Deborah Puntenney for helping to manage the project. Megan Mekinda and Kendra Alexander helped to analyze the qualitative data, and each coauthored a chapter in this book and reviewed several others (Megan also coauthored Appendix 1).

The study's scientific advisory board provided valuable insights on the evaluation's design and data analysis and in the preparation of the Technical Report on the overarching evaluation. I thank Jacquelynne Eccles, Greg Duncan, Denise Gottfredson, Robert Halpern, Stephen Hamilton, Reed Larson, Jeylan Mortimer, and Elizabeth Reisner for their expertise and guidance.

Many thanks to the William T. Grant Foundation, Wallace Foundation, and Searle Fund for funding the After School Matters evaluation. After School Matters provided a planning grant in the development stage of the study.

The job interview training program benefitted from the support of a number of individuals who held leadership positions at the time in Chicago Public Schools, including Adam Case, Aarti Dhupelia, and Jerusha Rogers. We are very grateful to the teachers who taught the curriculum, with special thanks to Kevin Rutter. At Northwestern, the project benefited from the creative involvement and commitment of Megan Mekinda, Rachel Hirsch, and Kendra Alexander. I am grateful to the William T. Grant Foundation for their continued funding.

A number of colleagues generously read earlier drafts of different chapters of this book, including Mesmin Destin, James Rosenbaum, and James Spillane. My thinking about these matters was enriched, especially about parallels to the situation of minorities in France, through discussions with sociology faculty at Sciences Po in Paris, where I presented a much condensed version of these findings.

Each member of my family contributed in a very specific way to this project. My son David, when he was in ninth grade, served as the first pilot subject for the mock job interview. My daughter Rachel coordinated the job interview training and taught the curriculum to a dance apprenticeship at After School Matters. My wife, Margherita Andreotti, generously brought to bear her professional editing skills on the penultimate draft of the manuscript. Of course, I am everlastingly grateful to them for their love and support.

I have dedicated this book to the memory of Maggie Daley. Prior to her death in 2011, Mrs. Daley was Chicago's First Lady, as the wife of Chicago's longtime mayor, Richard M. Daley. Mrs. Daley, who was widely admired for her graciousness, had an unwavering commitment to Chicago youth, especially those from disadvantaged communities. She cofounded gallery37, which evolved into After School Matters. She served continually as Chair of After School Matters and was no mere figurehead; Mrs. Daley was actively involved in all aspects of the program. The evaluation would not have been possible without her support.

There is one particular interaction that we had that left its mark on me. After a meeting in which early findings from the mock job interview were discussed, Mrs. Daley drew me aside for a brief, private conversation. In an earnest and heartfelt voice, she told me how much the program needed to improve and that she was counting on me to provide them with good answers for how to do so. Her words spoke to her vision and ambition, and to the kind of honest appraisal that is necessary to realize it. I hope that this book is responsive to her plea.

1

Preparing Youth for Work

Youth workforce development is an important policy objective under any circumstance. Young people need to be integrated into the workforce for the economy and society to function. It is a basic, fundamental need. In this era, several macro-level developments make this especially vital. Within most Western countries, the baby boom cohort is reaching retirement age and there is a need for new workers to take their place. Young workers are also necessary to keep social security systems solvent: the fewer young people in the workforce, paying into social security, the less funds will be available for the retired. On a global level, competitive forces have increased and a skilled workforce is essential for any country to maintain its position.

Nonetheless, integrating youth into the workforce is not easy, and the difficulties have been exacerbated by economies weakened by the Great Recession. Articles in major national publications such as *The New York Times* and *The Atlantic* highlight policymakers' attempts to combat soaring rates of youth unemployment in Europe.[1] In Italy, for example, for those younger than age twenty-five, the unemployment rate has topped 40 percent.

In the United States, which has recovered more quickly from economic setbacks than Europe, the youth unemployment rate is lower, approximately 16 percent, but this is still more than double the overall US unemployment rate. Minority youth have always had much higher unemployment rates than majority youth. At present, the official black youth unemployment rate in the United States is approximately 30 percent (and many consider this figure to be an underestimation, as it counts only those who are actively seeking employment). Early unemployment can "scar" youth and make obtaining employment as an adult more difficult, and consequently

---

[1] Ewing & Eddy (2013); Thompson (2013).

the developmental transition into adult life more problematic.[2] At age forty-two, wages may still be 13 to 21 percent less for those who experienced unemployment during their youth,[3] bringing hardship to individuals and families. Over the long term, these issues can tear at the social fabric of society.

Historically, a variety of social policies have sought to prepare youth to enter the workforce. Rather than review these exhaustively, we shall consider major systems in Europe and the United States.[4]

The German apprenticeship system is widely considered the "gold standard" in youth workforce development.[5] Germany has a dual education system that combines extensive on-the-job training (a minimum of three days each week) with at least one day per week in school. The on-the-job training is provided by designated, experienced workers and may include rotation among various jobs in a firm. The schools provide both general education (e.g., in German and social studies) as well as instruction geared toward developing understanding and skills for the work that youth are doing at a firm. There is an effort to integrate the academic material with applications in the workplace, so that subjects, such as math, are oriented toward the needs of specific occupations. Learning in school is designed to supplement what is learned on the job.

The German dual system is regulated by federal (national) law and involves cooperation among the government, employers, and unions (a state of affairs that is currently unimaginable in the US context). Apprenticeships normally last for three years. They are offered in 348 occupations, the majority in service sector jobs (60 percent) and the remainder in industrial production (40 percent). Almost a quarter of all German firms (24 percent) train apprentices and approximately two-thirds of youth complete an apprenticeship by age twenty-five. Nearly 60 percent of all apprentices are

---

[2] Bell & Blanchflower (2011); Gregg & Tominey (2005); Mroz & Savage (2006). Ellwood (1980) is an important early study. The broader area of minority youth unemployment has been of scholarly interest for several decades; see the excellent early collection of papers by Freeman & Holzer (1986).

[3] Gregg & Tominey (2005).

[4] For a report on European initiatives more broadly, see European Commission (2013) and reports from the Organisation for Economic Co-Operation and Development (e.g., OECD, 2010). There is also research on European and US samples that addresses the school-to-work transition outside of the policy and program context (see, e.g., papers in the anthologies by Neumark, 2007, and by Schoon & Silbereisen, 2009; also Ryan, 2001). For the developing world, see National Research Council & Institute of Medicine (2005).

[5] This discussion draws largely on Steadman (2010) and Hamilton (1990). For a more skeptical view, see Harhoff & Kane (1997).

subsequently employed by the firm in which they completed their apprenticeship. Related systems exist in Austria and Switzerland.[6]

In the United States, apprenticeship training is decidedly less popular.[7] Historians note that the US apprenticeship system had been significantly weakened by the end of the nineteenth century. Instead, the vocational school replaced the apprenticeship as the primary vehicle for workforce development training. The US government began funding vocational education in 1917 with the passage of the Smith–Hughes Act. Stand-alone vocational schools, or vocational tracks within comprehensive high schools, were often quite popular. As sociologist Kathryn Neckerman notes, in Chicago in 1925 almost 60 percent of high school diplomas were conferred for completion of two-year and four-year vocational programs. One of the best equipped vocational high schools in Chicago had an enrollment of 7,000 by 1930. However, African American students faced discrimination, both in enrolling in the more selective vocational schools and in entering trades.

There have been continual efforts to invigorate vocational high schools.[8] The most intensive, current effort to improve workforce development of in-school youth focuses on the creation of career academies within high schools. These schools are organized around a career theme and provide academic and technical curricula, work-based learning opportunities, and links to local employers. Findings from MDRC's experimental evaluation of nine academies suggest a number of positive outcomes.[9] In particular, male academy students earned more than their non-academy counterparts, with the highest impact among those most at risk for dropping out. Such gains were not evident among female students. Additional problems were noted, including a high attrition rate and reduced enrollment in academic courses. This type of whole-school reform is also costly and complex, making it difficult to implement well.[10]

---

[6] France, which does not have as extensive an apprenticeship system, has a high rate of youth unemployment (though not as high as that of Italy) (Cahuc, Carcillo, & Zimmerman, 2013).

[7] The discussion of the US experience draws heavily on Hamilton (1990), Kett (1977), Neckerman (2007), Douglas (1921), and Stull & Sanders (2003). For a more recent, positive perspective on the potential of US apprenticeships, see Halpern (2009).

[8] MDRC has conducted experimental evaluations of career academies that suggest their promise, especially for males (Kemple & Snipes, 2000; Kemple, 2008). See more general discussion of career academies by Stern (2003). For a consideration of contemporary career and technical education, see Stone & Lewis (2012).

[9] Kemple & Willner (2008).

[10] National Research Council (2003).

Other real or perceived shortcomings persist. Vocational high schools remain stigmatized for what is deemed to be an inferior education, leading to inferior jobs. Theorists on the political left have criticized schools for reproducing the social class system, and vocational schools are part of this critique.[11] During discussions in Chicago, top administrators in career and technical education bemoaned to me the lack of on-the-job training opportunities, such as internships, for vocational students.

Outside of schools, the United States has long relied on private sector employment for high school students as an informal system for providing work experience.[12] The vast majority of teenagers (80 to 90 percent) are employed at some point during the high school years, increasingly in the retail sector.[13] Part-time work can generate positive outcomes for youth, including increased confidence and time management ability, enhanced academic success, and later life advantages that spring from expanded networks.[14] Teenage work can increase wages, employment, and occupational status up to ten years later.[15] Among minority youth, those who do not work at all during high school are at the highest risk of dropping out.[16] For youth from low-income families, jobs can offer an alternative to patterns of neighborhood crime and unemployment and enable them to obtain skills and resources that may apply to better jobs in the future.[17] Jobs that are more challenging and develop skills are the most valuable, though many jobs for young people do not provide these types of experiences.[18]

Employment opportunities are not as readily available to low-income, urban youth, who are the focus of this book.[19] Young people who obtain such jobs as are available may also become subject to the ridicule of peers for working in some of these settings, such as fast food establishments.[20] Moreover, the jobs are designed to maximize the profits of firms rather than the training of youth.

---

[11] Bowles & Gintis (1976) is probably the best known of these critiques. Symonds, Schwarz, & Ferguson (2011) note that "For all its potential, CTE [Career and Technical Education] is often demeaned and disparaged, especially among the nation's elites." [p. 28].

[12] This is especially true in comparing the United States to other countries (e.g., Zemsky, 2003).

[13] Staff, Messersmith, & Schulenberg (2009). An excellent overview of adolescent work experiences is provided by Mortimer (2003).

[14] Mortimer (2003); Mortimer et al. (1996).

[15] Carr, Wright, & Brody (1996); Ruhm (1997).

[16] Tienda & Ahituv (1996).

[17] Newman (1999).

[18] Greenberger & Steinberg (1986); Mortimer (2003).

[19] Entwisle, Alexander, & Olson (2000); Newman (1999).

[20] Newman (1999).

Given the value attached to working, there have been a number of efforts by the federal government to improve workforce development of young people. Large sums were committed to such programs from 1977 to 1981, during the Carter presidency, under the Youth Employment and Demonstration Projects Act (YEDPA) of 1977. Programs ranged widely, including occupational skills training, labor market preparation (e.g., career exploration, job search assistance), temporary jobs, and job placement. Substantial funds were also dedicated to research and evaluation. A National Research Council study concluded that too much was implemented too soon:

> The YEDPA legislation created a program that combined too short a time schedule with too many different program elements and objectives. The demand to quickly implement the full range of elements impaired the quality of many of the programs. In addition, the pressure to obtain a wide range of research results on those programs within a short time compounded the problem and resulted, in many cases, in poor research on hastily constructed programs. It may be that the lack of proven effectiveness of many programs is due as much to the instability of the system as to the inherent nature of the programs.[21]

YEDPA expired once Ronald Reagan became president.

The School-to-Work Opportunities Act of 1994, an initiative of President Bill Clinton that was enacted into law with bipartisan support, was another major effort to rethink youth workforce development.[22] This act sought to make high school education more work based. It sought to promote the integration of school- and work-based learning, career majors, and internships or apprenticeships in firms. The legislation, by design, sunset (expired) in 2001. Given the time limits, restrained federal funding, and implementation problems, accomplishments were modest. Most efforts were limited, involving activities such as career awareness fairs and one-day job shadowing. More ambitious goals that involved participation in a comprehensive school-to-work program had minimal enrollments: only 2 percent in 1996 and 3 percent in 1998.

Whereas previous vocational initiatives had elicited criticism from the political left, the School-to-Work Opportunities Act became subject to severe criticism by the political right. A 1998 op-ed column in *The*

---

[21] Betsey, Hollister, & Papageorgiou (1985), p. 5. The quote was underlined in the original.

[22] This section has been informed by a series of excellent papers collected by Stull & Sanders (2003); see especially chapters by Stull; Hershey; Schug & Western; Rosenbaum; Lerman; and Kazis & Pennington For a review of a wider range of employment related programs for low-income youth, see Edelman, Holzer, & Offner (2006), chapter 3.

New York Times by conservative intellectual Lynne Cheney, who had previously served as Chair of the National Endowment for the Humanities in the administrations of Ronald Reagan and George H. W. Bush, took the school-to-work movement to task.[23] Dr. Cheney began innocently enough:

> Almost everyone agrees that schools need to do a better job of preparing students for the workplace. So the "school to work" programs now up and running in 37 states should be uncontroversial. Keeping employer needs in mind and preparing students to meet them, as these programs intend, seem sensible things for schools to do.

She then attacks the law for overinclusiveness, government intrusiveness, and foreclosing ambitions at too early an age,

> Instead of focusing on students in vocational education ... school-to-work programs, by law, include all students. And in practice, the programs assume unwarranted authority over their children's lives.... Redirecting schools to prepare students for jobs that central planners recommend does not guarantee the economic well-being of those students, and can even be a hindrance. A student whose high school career focuses on specific jobs in one field may discover in college that another area is more interesting and therefore more likely to inspire high achievement. But early specialization leaves such a student unprepared to take the courses that his or her more mature aspirations require.

Cheney concludes with an endorsement of the liberal arts and their value, as opposed to a vocational thrust,

> Schools prepare citizens as well as workers, and they do so best when students are encouraged to read literature and history not merely for what they tell about the workplace, but for their insights into the human condition.

This op-ed is cited by some of those in the school-to-work field as being highly influential in undermining support for the movement. In the years to come, Dr. Cheney would achieve considerable visibility as the wife of Dick Cheney, vice president of the United States under George W. Bush.

In the years since the expiration of the act, the government has increasingly focused on promoting college for all. Nevertheless, many young people do not go to college. There is a very high dropout rate in community colleges, a frequent destination of urban minority youth.[24] Recent reports

---

[23] Cheney (1998). It has been noted that the German system also imposes a number of constraints on youth (Mortimer & Kruger, 2000).

[24] Rosenbaum (2001).

by the Consortium for Chicago School Research indicate just how few youth from low-income urban settings actually obtain a college degree. Their initial estimate, in 2006, was that only 8 percent of students who began high school in the Chicago Public Schools (CPS) district earn a four-year degree by the time they are in their mid-twenties. A more recent, 2014 estimate upped this figure to 14 percent, reflecting in large part an increase in the high school graduation rate.[25] Despite this gain, the problem of preparing youth for the workforce has clearly not gone away. Given the real and perceived shortcomings of vocational schools and majors, and the disappointment over the School-to-Work Opportunities Act, where will we find new possibilities to help promote youth workforce development, especially among the low-income minority groups who experience the most unemployment?

NEW PROGRAM DIRECTIONS

Various nonprofit organizations have initiated after-school programs in the United States that may help to address this gap. These programs received a considerable boost with federal funding of 21st Century Community Learning Centers during the Clinton presidency. The legislation itself was originally authored by Republicans and has received continued bipartisan support. Most after-school programs serve elementary and middle school children, but there has been increased attention to high school youth, particularly in urban areas. To make them attractive to adolescents, these new programs have increasingly focused on job-related skills and experiences, consistent with an emphasis on positive youth development. Youth can participate in these work-oriented after-school programs while still pursuing a college preparatory course of study, countering objections from both the right and the left to vocational tracks in school.

Chicago's After School Matters (ASM) is widely considered the flagship program for developing job skills among high school youth and is being emulated in several cities across the country. Targeted at students in CPS, ASM enrolled approximately 7,500 youth each semester in 2009 and is thought to be the largest program of its kind in the country. The program

---

[25] The first report actually gave a rate of 6 percent (Roderick, Nagaoka, & Allensworth, 2006), but more complete data from the University of Illinois at Urbana-Champaign led to a recalculation that put the estimate at 8 percent (Allensworth, 2006). The 2014 estimate is provided by Healey, Nagaoka, & Michelman (2014). It should be noted that the Consortium calculates high school graduation rates slightly differently than does CPS, given differences in coding out-of-district transfers.

takes place in school, after the conclusion of the regular school day. It is rare for sessions to take place at work sites, though it happens occasionally (Chapter 4). During the time of our research, youth were paid a stipend equivalent to $5 per hour if they met program attendance criteria.

ASM began as gallery37 in 1991, at which time it focused on the arts. In 2000, it began offering experiences in a much wider array of fields and changed its name to After School Matters. ASM had been found promising in a quasi-experimental study of academic outcomes, as well as in qualitative studies of a more diverse set of outcomes by leading researchers on after-school programs.[26]

The program offers ten-week experiences per semester (three hours per day, three days per week) in what are termed "apprenticeships." These are project-based experiences centered on the development and utilization of trade or artistic skills. Each apprenticeship is organized around a particular enterprise, which ranges widely in focus. Examples include apprenticeships focused exclusively on technology, such as Web design or computer repair; others that combine technology and art, such as producing social documentaries; still others that are primarily artistic, such as improvisational theater groups or dance; and finally ones that have a sports orientation, such as lifeguard training or learning how to teach young children to play soccer. Each apprenticeship session involves work in the designated area, learning and making use of relevant skills to accomplish specified tasks. Instructors provide information, guidance, and feedback and introduce students to the standards, language, and culture of that line of work.[27] The apprenticeship culminates in a final product or performance, which involves some public presentation.

Two paid instructors direct each apprenticeship. The instructors (who are typically not teachers) have expertise in – and in many instances earn their livelihood through – the activity that is the focus of the apprenticeship. ASM provides both beginning and advanced training sessions for instructors. Because after-school programs are not subject to school curricular requirements, the instructors have the flexibility to spend much more time on projects than is available in schools, potentially facilitating deep learning, a major goal of educational reformers. ASM experiences bear a familial-like resemblance to other apprenticeship-type interventions that

---

[26] The quasi-experimental study was by Goerge et al. (2007). The qualitative studies were by Halpern (2006) and Larson (2007). A more detailed account of these earlier studies is provided in Appendix 1.

[27] Halpern (2006).

provide exposure to work skills or environments in a particular occupation. They do not, however, provide the kind of intensive, on-the-job training in technical trade skills such as is found in Germany.[28]

ASM apprenticeships, in theory, reflect a number of design principles that are consistent with project-based learning. Youth work on authentic tasks that have meaning in the "real world," and they learn by doing.[29] The tasks are challenging in that they are often slightly beyond the youth's present ability yet manageable with assistance, what the Russian psychologist Lev Vygotsky would refer to as the zone of proximal development.[30] Instructors provide scaffolding and guided feedback.[31] Youth are encouraged to take initiative, make decisions, and be creative, and they are provided opportunities to teach or share what they have learned with their peers.[32] Finally, tasks and skills are developed sequentially so that proximal goals map logically onto distal objectives, and the final product/performance demands consideration of everything (or almost everything) that the youth have learned.[33]

This book reports a series of research investigations that began with a random assignment evaluation of ASM and culminated in the development of a job interview training program that was implemented in CPS. The findings that are reported in the book focus on ASM's ability to provide effective youth workforce development. There are several distinct strengths of the evaluation that are reflected in this book.

First, the ASM research involved a true experimental evaluation (otherwise known as a randomized controlled trial), which is rare in either evaluations of workforce development or after-school programs, particularly for programs involving youth who are still in high school.[34] Randomization is the best procedure for guarding against selection effects in which youth more likely to improve over time are disproportionately located in the treatment group. In that event, it is impossible to sort out whether effects are due to selection (who got into the program) or the program itself (the experiences of youth while in the program). This is why randomized controlled trials are typically considered the "gold standard" in evaluation research.

[28] See Hamilton (1990) for an account of German apprenticeships.
[29] Edelson (2001); Schank (1995).
[30] Vygotsky (1978).
[31] Jackson, Krajcik, & Soloway (1998); Rogoff, 1990).
[32] Barron (1998); Brown & Campione (1996).
[33] Brown & Campione (1996).
[34] Mekinda (2014).

Second, the assessment of youth's marketable job skills was centered on a mock job interview created for this research. The interview was administered, for enhanced credibility, by experienced human resource (HR) professionals (the interview is discussed in detail in Chapter 2).

Third, a mixed-methods approach was utilized, with extensive analysis of both quantitative and qualitative data. The quantitative data from the mock job interview were analyzed using advanced statistical procedures (hierarchical linear modeling). In terms of qualitative data, we observed each apprenticeship once a week (three hours) and detailed fieldnotes were taken by our trained observers (who were mostly graduate students). We have approximately 2,400 pages of fieldnotes; in addition, the observer of each apprenticeship completed an extensive case study of that apprenticeship. Anchored by quantitative findings on hiring rates from the mock job interview, the qualitative data enabled us to shed light on the "black box" of what happened in the programs. We consider these fieldnotes in Chapter 3, where we contrast the two best- and the two worst-performing apprenticeships as defined by youth hiring rates versus their control groups on the mock job interview. The fieldnotes are also analyzed in Chapter 4, where we consider two of ASM's best apprenticeships; these two implemented the overall ASM approach differently, and we consider which is most likely to be successfully implemented by other programs. Thus, we use the qualitative data to learn much more from our evaluation of ASM than would be available exclusively from the quantitative data.

Finally, I should note that although most evaluation studies are at best weakly tied to developmental theory, this was not the case with our studies. The research drew on cultural and ecological approaches to adolescent development. I have taught graduate courses on adolescent development for more than twenty years. A developmental approach enables us to situate and understand the findings in terms of the tasks, knowledge, competencies, and relationships of adolescents, and the types of supports that facilitate development.

In the remainder of this chapter, I provide more specifics about two new program directions. The first part provides more detail about ASM and, especially, about our evaluation methodology. The second part introduces a new program that we developed that grew out of what our HR professionals told us about how youth performed in the mock job interview (the HR findings are presented in Chapter 5 and the new program is presented in Chapter 6). These insights pertain particularly to how youth can more effectively recognize and communicate the relevance of their accomplishments in job interviews. The insights address a major developmental skill that has not been discussed in the literature and that could have an important impact on hiring rates of low-income, minority youth.

AN OVERVIEW OF THE ASM EVALUATION METHODOLOGY

The ASM evaluation focused on thirteen apprenticeships that were located in ten Chicago public high schools. Among these ten schools, the four-year average graduation rate was 57 percent (ranging from 30 to 69 percent). The average percentage of students passing the eleventh grade statewide achievement tests was 18 percent (ranging from 3 to 40 percent). Seven schools were majority African American and three schools were majority Latino.

Apprenticeship selection focused on experienced instructors who had a history of implementing the ASM model well and a strong orientation to youth skill development. There was a special concern to avoid instructors (particularly in the arts) who might be charismatic but not adhere strongly to the program model. We had ASM program directors nominate several of the best programs from their region according to these criteria. Some nominees declined to participate and some others withdrew prior to program onset for personal or family reasons. The final group of apprenticeships in the evaluation was considered among the better ones in ASM but not the very best exclusively. Each had site visit ratings (conducted by ASM staff), data from ASM youth exit surveys (completed by former apprentices), and program attendance records that were reasonably consistent with our criteria. All instructors had at least one year of ASM experience. The content of the apprenticeships varied widely, from the artistic (e.g., African drumming and dance, songwriting and producing) to the technological (e.g., creating mock retail websites, repairing computer hard drives).

Choosing the better ASM apprenticeships was intended to minimize implementation issues and give ASM the "best chance" to demonstrate impact. At the same time, choosing the better apprenticeships limited the potential generalizability of the findings as the apprenticeships that were evaluated were not representative of the typical ASM apprenticeship.[35] Furthermore, although ASM typically has youth enroll semester by semester,

---

[35] In public health terms, studying the better apprenticeships is consistent with an efficacy study; however, ASM instructors were not provided with feedback or supervision beyond what they would ordinarily receive, which is consistent with an effectiveness study.

each of these thirteen apprenticeships required youth to sign up for two consecutive semesters for purposes of more meaningful evaluation.

Randomization was at the level of the individual. In the usual scenario, the two instructors for each apprenticeship would go to the high school at the beginning of the term, set up a table, and talk about the apprenticeship with any student who stopped by. Interested youth were interviewed by the instructors. Instructors could decline to accept a youth, which meant that the identified youth did not make it into our subject pool and was thus ineligible to participate in the study in any capacity. We then randomly selected from this subject pool who would be in the apprenticeship (treatment) group and who would be in the control group. The research team used an SPSS computer program to make the actual selection. This approach equated the groups for motivation and interest in the topic of the apprenticeship, as well as in youth's initial appraisal of the apprenticeship instructors.

Youth in the control group could pursue any other after-school program or activity as they normally would ("business as usual"), with the exception that they could not enter another ASM apprenticeship. The overwhelming majority of the control group (91 percent) reported involvement either in an organized after-school activity (primarily) or paid work. Most of these were on a sports team (33 percent) or in a performance, music, or art program (25 percent). Thus, we were effectively comparing ASM to an alternative treatment. It is much harder to demonstrate impact when there is an alternative treatment rather than no-treatment as the comparison.

A seven-item survey questionnaire was developed to assess relatively objective design features of either the apprenticeship (for the apprenticeship youth) or the most time-intensive extracurricular activity (for youth in the control group). Items were chosen to assess key features of the ASM program model (program fidelity or integrity). For example, youth rated "How often did an adult leader teach you some skills while you were involved in this activity?" and "How often did you have a deadline to accomplish something in this activity?"[36] Youth in ASM apprenticeships reported significantly higher scores on this measure than did youth in the control group, reflecting that the apprenticeships were perceived by youth to adhere more closely to the ASM program model.[37]

---

[36] The seven-item scale had an internal reliability $\alpha = .76$.

[37] Youth in the treatment group reported a significantly higher scale mean ($M = 4.39$, $SD = .62$) on the design features measure than the control group ($M = 3.80$, $SD = .70$), with a treatment effect of nearly one standard deviation ($F = 42.77$, Hedges $g = .89$, $p < .01$). Youth in treatment reported the instructors were more likely to teach them a skill, how to improve their skills, and how the activities were related to a job. The apprentices

Preparing Youth for Work

Data were collected over a three-year period (2006–2009). A total of 535 high school youth were included in the evaluation.[38] Most were freshmen or sophomores (66 percent), female (59 percent), African American (77 percent), or Latino (23 percent), and were from low-income families (92 percent) as determined by receipt of subsidized school lunches. There were no significant differences between ASM and the control group on any demographic variable (nor on standardized test performance as averaged over their two most recent tests). Additional details on the methodology are provided in Appendix 1, as well as in our technical report on the evaluation.[39]

This book focuses on that portion of the ASM evaluation that was concerned with marketable job skills. The broader evaluation also considered impacts on positive youth development; school attitude, grades, and attendance; and problem behaviors; for interested readers, those findings are reported and discussed in Appendix 1.

It is important to recognize that our evaluation findings reflect ASM during the specific time period of our research. In the years since then, there has been a substantial turnover of top administrators and a variety of changes in programs and staff training. This report, thus, is more an evaluation of a type of program rather than some cast-in-stone model of ASM.

---

also rated having a deadline, being able to make choices related to the activity, and working on a project that was used or viewed by others as happening more often than what the control group reported for their activities.

[38] There were 304 youth assigned to treatment, 231 assigned to control. An explanation of the different size of the groups is in order.

In the first year, we selected up to fifty youth per apprenticeship (twenty-five intervention and twenty-five control) who completed the qualification procedures. We increased our target enrollment to fifty-six per apprenticeship (twenty-eight intervention and twenty-eight control) in year 2 and to sixty per apprenticeship (thirty intervention and thirty control) in year 3, to address treatment attrition. Although *all* subjects were randomly assigned, if an apprenticeship did not reach the target enrollment at the time of the lottery, we instructed the SPSS random number generator to assign more subjects to treatment than control. In addition, for apprenticeships that had a large number of no-shows, we conducted a second lottery by randomly selecting up to five youth initially assigned to the control group to be reassigned to treatment. The second lottery occurred no later than the second week of the apprenticeship. These procedures maintained the integrity of the experimental design while also enabling the apprenticeships to meet ASM enrollment requirements, a major system-wide concern of the organization during the second and third years of the study.

The assignment of more subjects to the intervention than the control group was the principal factor leading to the differential size of the groups. The differential assignment was modest. For example, consider that if we had changed the assignment ratio so that on average, per apprenticeship, we assigned three fewer youth to the treatment group than to the control group (relative to our actual assignments), the resulting size of the treatment group would have been 265 and the control group size would have been 270.

[39] Hirsch et al. (2011).

To emphasize this, henceforth I will refer not to "After School Matters" or "ASM," but rather to ASM2009, which represents the last year of our data collection.

A SECOND NEW PROGRAM DIRECTION

Beginning with our initial mock job interviews during the first year of the evaluation, we debriefed the HR interviewers. We talked with them about their impressions of youth employability and asked whether there were any distinctive aspects to the youth in each specific school or any other topic that they wanted to discuss. During the first year, these debriefing sessions were done casually. It took me a while to understand and appreciate fully how HR professionals thought and why certain things were important to them. As the study proceeded, we devoted more time to these debriefing sessions and began to tape and transcribe them. I also discussed the initial findings from the debriefing sessions with colleagues from different disciplines and identified a set of questions to address more systematically during the debriefings.

In Chapter 5, we discuss our major findings from these debriefings. It became clear that the HR interviewers believed that many of the young people had experiences and skills that would be valuable to employers. However, based on a mistaken understanding of what is job relevant, youth often did not bring their credentials up during the interview or did so in a manner that was not convincing to the interviewer.

At the request of top administrators in CPS, we then developed a program to help high school youth identify and communicate their work-related competencies. As part of this effort, we convened a group of HR interviewers from the ASM2009 study and discussed in detail with them what youth needed to know to do well in job interviews. The program that resulted from this effort, along with promising initial evaluation results, is presented in Chapter 6.

The concluding chapter of the book, Chapter 7, discusses what we learned from these varied initiatives and evaluations. We identify priorities to guide policy and the next generation of programs.

2

Do Youth in After School Matters Have
More Marketable Job Skills?

One of the primary goals of After School Matters (ASM2009) was to develop marketable job skills among the youth enrolled in their apprenticeships. Positive youth development was ASM2009's top goal, but marketable job skills came second. The belief that youth developed marketable job skills was trumpeted in program publicity, being featured on websites and in announcements during large public performances. Top ASM2009 leaders repeatedly made the importance of this goal clear to me in our meetings. ASM2009 could have described their goal as the development of job skills, but they did not. It was always marketable job skills. So what makes a job skill *marketable*?

Marketable job skills would seem to be skills that you can successfully market or sell to employers, that convince them you can do the job. Having job skills that are marketable means that an employer would be willing to hire you on the basis of those skills.

The employment interview is the principal method by which employers assess job skills and make hiring decisions. Even social scientists who prefer that employers base such decisions on other kinds of data recognize that employers rely heavily on job interviews. For instance, sociologist James Rosenbaum preferred that decisions on whether to employ youth be based on school performance and teacher recommendations; nonetheless, in a study of employers who hire entry-level workers, he admitted that

> All fifty-one employers we interviewed lean heavily on the information that they can gather themselves by directly interviewing applicants; all of the employers we spoke with rely on interviews. ... In sum, interviews are the primary determinant of hiring. From interviews, employers believe that they can infer which applicants have the requisite attitude,

[and] interpersonal skills ... Employers believe that they can make broad inferences from interviews, even if they last only fifteen minutes.[1]

Skills assessed during job interviews, moreover, predict later evaluations of actual job performance.[2]

We could not, of course, convince real employers to make 500 or so jobs available so that youth participating in our research could interview for them. These would have to be mock jobs. No mock job interview for high school students existed at the time we planned our evaluation and so we would have to develop one ourselves. Developing assessment procedures is something that psychologists such as myself are trained to do – and, I must admit, often enjoy as well. So let us consider the various factors that went into the design of the mock job interview before discussing the evaluation findings.

DEVELOPMENT OF THE MOCK JOB INTERVIEW

The design of the mock job interview was not entirely a straightforward proposition. Each of these issues was important:

- Who should design the mock job interview?
- What job should youth apply for?
- Who should conduct the interviews?
- What questions should be asked in the interview? How should youth responses be rated?
- Is the instrument methodologically sound according to common criteria?
- When should the interviews take place?

Let us consider each of these in turn.

---

[1] Rosenbaum (2001), quotes are from pp. 141 and 144. See also Holzer (1996); Lievens, Highhouse, & De Corte (2005); Macan (2009); Moss & Tilly (2001); and Topor, Colarelli, & Han (2007) on the importance of interviews in hiring. Eder & Harris (1999), a handbook, is a good resource for information on employment interviews. The employment interview is the most popular selection technique in Europe as well as the United States (Dipboye, Macan, & Shahani-Denning, 2012).

[2] Berry, Sackett, & Landers (2007); DeGroot & Motowidlo (1999); Dipboye et al. (2012); Huffcutt (2011); Huffcutt et al. (2001); Huffcutt & Roth (1998); Macan (2009). The most recent review (Levashina et al., 2014) indicates that validities seem to be higher for structured interviews that use standardized questions and anchored rating scales (which is what we used). There is growing support for the use of interviews as measures of noncognitive skills.

Who Should Design the Mock Job Interview?

The mock job interview needed to be a good proxy for the real thing. In employment contexts, this is the domain of human resource (HR) professionals. Having an HR voice in the design seemed essential. I also participated to contribute methodological expertise and to facilitate collaboration among the HR professionals. Two senior, local HR professionals played the most important role in the design: one operated her own HR consulting practice, and the other was HR manager for a global firm with headquarters in Chicago (in the text that follows I refer to them as our HR consultants). The three of us worked collaboratively in the development of the mock job interview and both of them gave the final instrument their professional blessing. The Northwestern Mock Job Interview is reproduced in Appendix 2.

What Job Should Youth Apply for?

This was not a simple issue. An initial thought might be to have the youth apply for a job in the field of their apprenticeship. After all, they are learning technical skills for that type of work (e.g., how to do digital photography using high-end software). But this option was not tenable for the control group. Almost all of them, as indicated in Chapter 1, were in an organized after-school activity, and could be gaining marketable job skills from that involvement, but they were in all kinds of different activities. It wouldn't be a fair comparison if we forced control youth to apply for a job, let us say, in digital photography, and compared them to ASM2009 youth who had just had an apprenticeship in that area. That would bias the results in favor of ASM2009. Moreover, we know that most youth in vocational programs in high school do not intend to seek jobs in that occupation post-school and we assumed that this would apply to ASM2009 as well[3]; presumably ASM2009 youth would want to develop job skills that would be useful more broadly and not just in the field of their apprenticeship.

Given the direction of our overall economy, we thought that service jobs would be most available to young people and would be attractive to them. This is consistent with research by economist Harry Holzer, who found that the majority of jobs available to less educated workers, particularly in cities like Chicago, were in the retail and service sectors.[4]

---

[3] Stone & Lewis (2012).
[4] Holzer (1996).

Our HR consultants told us that in hiring for those jobs, employers focused less on technical skills, which they often preferred to teach themselves according to their own methods.[5] Instead, the focus was on work readiness and soft skills: demonstrating respect for others and responsiveness to supervision, critical thinking, analytical ability, problem solving, initiative, teamwork, leadership, communication skills, and so on. Corporate leaders have repeatedly highlighted the need for these more generic skills that are useful for almost every job.[6]

We also wanted to have some variety in the types of jobs that youth could interview for, but not too much. If there were many possible jobs, then there could be differences in how easy or difficult it would be to demonstrate suitable credentials in the interview; we would not, for example, want ASM2009 youth to apply for jobs that were easier to talk about in the job interview and control youth to apply for the harder jobs.

Bearing these different considerations in mind, we ultimately offered three jobs that had nearly identical specifications. Pilot interviews revealed that each of these was attractive to Chicago teenagers. One job involved working at the United Center (home of the Chicago Bulls professional basketball team), another involved working in Millennium Park, a highly popular new park in downtown Chicago, and the third involved working at Chicago Cool Clothes, a retail establishment that we made up for the purpose of the interview. The description of each job was similar and involved a variety of experiences: customer service, set-up and take-down of displays, and office work. This allowed the youth choice in the job for which they would interview and an opportunity to discuss any specific skill, among several listed, in which they had experience or interest in developing. We defined the mock jobs as summer jobs. We thought that would make them more accessible to the young people, many of whom were freshmen or sophomores in high school.

Who Should Conduct the Interviews?

Logistically, it would have been easiest if the interviews were conducted by graduate students working on the evaluation. They were readily available for training and could be easily scheduled. Many research projects follow that route. But we could imagine that interviews conducted by social science graduate students might have less than ideal credibility outside

[5] See also Hamilton (1990); Moss & Tilly (2001); Whalen, DeCoursey, & Skyles (2003).
[6] Casner-Lotto & Barrington (2006); Conrad (1999); Moss & Tilly (1996).

the university. After all, wouldn't university researchers, because of their (presumed) values, be willing to hire just about any low-income, minority youth? For the findings to be credible in the business and policy worlds, and considered trustworthy by those who might be inclined to doubt, we had the interviews conducted by experienced HR professionals. A total of twenty-eight HR professionals gave their time pro bono and conducted the interviews over the course of three years.[7]

What Questions Should Be Asked in the Interview? How Should Youth Responses Be Rated?

Prior reviews of research on job interviews indicated that most interviews are composed of both behavioral and situational questions. Behavioral questions probe what an interviewee did in a prior situation ("Tell me about a time when …"). This allows interviewers to examine actions and thought processes in actual prior situations. Situational questions inquire as to what an interviewee would do in a hypothetical situation ("What would you do if …"). I discussed these two alternatives with a senior social scientist who had authored important reviews of this literature, as well as with our HR collaborators. All of them felt that it would on balance be useful to include both types of questions. The HR consultants then selected a total of thirteen questions that were common in job interviews. As per usual HR practice, interviewers would be allowed to probe youth answers. Probes were permitted as long as they asked all thirteen questions within the maximum twenty-minute time period.

Immediately on conclusion of the twenty-minute interview, the interviewers had a feedback session with each youth. The feedback emphasized youth strengths in the interview and suggested areas or approaches that youth might use in future, real job interviews. It often happened that additional information surfaced during these feedback sessions. This additional information was brought to my attention during debriefing of the HR interviewers and proved very critical in helping us to understand youth employability. These qualitative data are presented in detail in Chapter 5. However, none of the information obtained during the feedback session could be

---

[7] The day of the first round of interviews, at the last minute two HR interviewers were unable to come. As we had planned for only one possible no-show, this put us in a bind. Accordingly, I personally conducted three of the interviews on that day, but was not informed as to which of those youth were in the ASM2009 versus control group. All of the other interviews in the project were conducted by HR professionals. For subsequent interview days, we scheduled to allow for the possibility of two HR no-shows.

used in making subsequent ratings; if we had allowed the interviewers to use this additional information to inform their ratings, it would have altered the interview and made it much less like a real interview, diminishing its validity.[8]

After the youth left the interview room, each of the thirteen interview questions was then rated on a 1–5 scale. A brief description was given for ratings of 1, 3, and 5 to anchor the scale according to specific criteria. The HR consultants defined the criteria and modified them as they conducted pilot interviews and considered youth responses. The consultants sought to make the criteria reflect what HR interviewers would look for if this were an actual hiring situation.

In addition to rating the thirteen interview questions (which we termed the "A" items, as they came first), we also had the HR interviewers rate thirteen additional items of a more global sort (which we termed the "B" items). These focused on initial impressions made by the interviewee; amount of eye contact; and overall judgments about communication skills, maturity, and so on. Two of these latter thirteen ratings specified whether the young person would be hired for the job. One asked whether the youth would be hired for a summer job and the other whether the youth would be hired for a permanent job. Because they were so important to our research, we defined each of the 1–5 ratings for the hiring items in terms of how HR professionals actually think about this decision:

1. I would definitely not hire this applicant.
2. It is unlikely I would hire this applicant.
3. I see enough potential in this applicant that I might hire them if I really needed someone. ("Hold Box").
4. This applicant meets the job criteria and I would be willing to hire them.
5. I am enthusiastic about this applicant and would definitely hire them.

For a youth to be considered "hired" in our research, he or she needed to be rated either 4 or 5.

We expected that the hiring ratings would be made on the basis of how well youth were rated in the areas tapped by the A and B items. To test this statistically, we formed scales based on all of the A items and on all of the B

---

[8] In actual HR practice, it happens from time to time that interviewers are made aware of information that is privileged and that they are not allowed to use. Thus, our interviewers had already been trained as part of their profession to disregard the type of additional information obtained during the feedback session, and we explicitly reinforced this necessity.

items. Using as a sample all youth who participated in the mock job interview (both ASM2009 and control youth), we found that both the A scale ($r = .69$) and the B scale ($r = .86$) correlated significantly with the measure of hiring for a permanent job (our most stringent hiring measure).

Is the Instrument Methodologically Sound According to Common Criteria?

We wanted to make sure that there would be reasonable agreement among interviewers, which we decided would be at least 80 percent.[9] To make sure that we achieved this, our two HR consultants developed consensus ratings for each of the A and B items for two videotaped, pilot interviews. One of these was with a young man who did well in the interview, another was with a young woman who did poorly.

The next step was to determine whether each of our potential HR interviewers were able to agree on 80 percent or more of the items with the consensus codes. The training involved familiarizing potential interviewers with the mock job interview and ratings. We went over each question and possible rating in detail. The potential interviewers then viewed the first tape and discussed their ratings (they enjoyed this "shop talk" with other professionals). They then viewed the second tape and, again, made and discussed their ratings. All of the interviewers met the interrater agreement criterion. The videotape and discussion also helped to give them models of how the semistructured interviews might be conducted and get them used to seeing teenagers in an employment interview context.

We also examined the internal reliability of the two scales (which essentially measures how well the items consistently go together). Both the A scale ($\alpha = .76$) and the B scale ($\alpha = .91$) had adequate internal reliability.

When Should the Interviews Take Place?

Ideally, we would have liked to conduct both preintervention and postintervention interviews with both ASM2009 and control group youth. However, all youth needed to complete a number of time-consuming tasks prior to the beginning of the apprenticeships. This included completing our Web-based assessment battery, an interview with the ASM2009 instructors, return of signed parental consent and youth assent forms, and so on. Getting all of

---

[9] In social science, this is referred to as interrater reliability. In the HR world, this is referred to as calibration.

these done in a very short period of time proved quite challenging. It would have been logistically impossible to have conducted mock job interviews at this time as well.[10] Fortunately, given that the youth were randomly assigned to groups, it was not necessary to have a preintervention assessment to use findings from the postintervention mock job interview.

QUANTITATIVE RESULTS FROM THE EVALUATION

As discussed in Chapter 1, the evaluation was a randomized controlled trial or experimental evaluation. Youth interested in participating in a specific ASM2009 apprenticeship were randomly assigned by the research team to either that apprenticeship or the control condition ("business as usual"). It turned out that 91 percent of control youth participated in some other organized after-school activity, so they were more like an alternative treatment condition rather than a no-treatment condition. Accordingly, this meant that we were investigating whether ASM2009 added value above and beyond what could be found in an alternative after-school activity.

The mock job interview took place, for both ASM2009 and control youth, at their high school on a spring Saturday, around the time that the ten-week spring apprenticeship came to an end. After completing an extensive Web-based assessment of other measures related to the broader evaluation, 444 young people then participated in the mock job interview. Each interview was between an individual HR professional and an individual youth. The interviewers were dressed in business attire.[11] The interviews were held in empty classrooms.

---

[10] ASM2009 had severe time restrictions as to when recruitment could start and when the apprenticeships needed to begin. In addition to what needed to be accomplished to get students ready for apprenticeships and our study, there would have been additional, serious logistical issues in scheduling the HR interviewers over a very short time span.

[11] There was considerable discussion regarding the standard of attire to be expected of the student interviewees. On the one hand, interviewers do evaluate an applicant's appearance, and generally job candidates dress reasonably well for a job interview. On the other hand, we did not want some of our youth research participants not to show up because they did not want to "dress up." All of the interviews took place on a Saturday in the springtime, often on a warm, sunny day after a long Chicago winter. Many youth had to take public transportation to get to school on the weekend, which could take a good amount of time. Many of them would engage in recreational activities immediately afterward. All of these factors worked against their attending the assessment at all. We were very concerned that some youth would not show up – decreasing the value of the entire evaluation – if they felt that the dress code was too much of an additional burden. Ultimately, we decided that we expected the young people to be dressed "neatly" and they were so informed when given their appointment time. The HR interviewers took this as their standard regarding appearance.

The research team assigned an approximately equal number of ASM2009 and control youth to each interviewer. Every effort was made to prevent the HR interviewers from being biased in favor of reporting greater hiring rates for the ASM2009 youth. The interviewer was not told before the interview whether the youth had been participating in ASM2009; indeed, 21 percent of control youth had participated in ASM in a prior year. Although the interviewers were aware that the study involved ASM2009, I told them that we were most interested in the pattern of experiences (e.g., school, extra-curricular and volunteer experiences, part-time jobs) that best predicted eventual youth employability. I emphasized that if they had any belief as to what the research team hoped to find, they should disregard that, for if they acted on that belief all of their data – and involvement – would be useless. Finally, I stressed that above all they were to act professionally, that they should treat the youth as actual potential hires, and that they should act as if they would be held personally responsible by the firm's supervisors for their hiring recommendations, just as they would in real life.

We used hierarchical linear modeling (HLM) to analyze whether there were statistically significant differences between ASM2009 and control group youth on the interview ratings. Although the randomization proce-dure is the best way to ensure that there is equivalence between the groups, we also examined a number of control variables to make sure we eliminated any potential differences that existed prior to randomization. Including these control variables also increased our statistical power to detect between-group differences that may exist. The control variables included race, gender, socioeconomic status, age, prior work experience, prior extra-curricular involvement, and prior participation in an ASM program.[12]

Two sets of analyses were conducted. The first is technically termed intent-to-treat. In these analyses, the groups are defined by all youth who were originally assigned to either ASM2009 or the control group, regardless of whether they participated in ASM2009 or dropped out. Methodologists consider this to be the strongest test of whether one group is different from the other as it preserves the original randomization.

The second set of analyses is technically referred to as treatment-on-the-treated. In these analyses, ASM2009 youth are not included if they failed to show up for the apprenticeship, dropped out of their assigned appren-ticeship, or did not meet ASM2009's attendance threshold (73 percent of

---

[12] Apprenticeship selection is considered a fixed effect, as noted in Appendix 1. Further details are provided in Appendix 1 and in Hirsch et al. (2011). I am grateful to Larry V. Hedges, who directed these statistical analyses.

sessions). We also excluded control subjects who managed to enroll in an alternative ASM2009 apprenticeship despite our best efforts to prevent this. We did not detect any significant demographic differences between the treated ASM2009 group and the control group. However, as noted in Appendix 1, youth who remained in the treatment group reported marginally higher self-efficacy ($p = .093$) prior to assignment than youth in the control group.

Intent-to-Treat Results

The results of these analyses can be summarized quite succinctly: there was no mock job interview variable on which there was a statistically significant difference between ASM2009 and control group youth. As can be seen in Table 2.1, this included the hiring variables, an index of all of the A items that measured performance on specific interview questions, and an index of the B variables that measured overall interviewee characteristics (communication skills, maturity, etc.).[13] A significance level of .05 was utilized in all statistical analyses in our research.

Treatment-on-the-Treated Results

The results of these analyses are slightly more favorable to ASM2009. Once again, though, as seen in Table 2.2, there was no statistically significant difference on the hiring variables between youth in ASM2009 and those in the control group. However, there was a statistically significant difference on the composite scale of A items, and a marginally significant difference on the composite scale of the B items, both of which favored ASM2009.

We then examined scores on the individual items that made up each subscale. If there were significant differences on items of substantive importance, then this would suggest that ASM2009 could be having a meaningful impact that had yet to show up on the hiring variables or the intent-to-treat analyses. However, this was not the case. There was only one item on the A scale that was statistically significant, and that was an item that tapped how the young person would deal with a disagreement with his or her supervisor. In the real world, this is not a trivial issue. But most of our

---

[13] We also conducted sensitivity analyses to see whether African American males, and low socioeconomic status groups, were differentially impacted by participation in ASM2009 versus the control group. Again, there were no statistically significant differences (Hirsch, Hedges et al., 2011).

TABLE 2.1 *Marketable job skills: Intent-to-treat comparison*

	ASM2009 N = 262 M (SD)	Control N = 182 M (SD)	Effect size (g)	Treatment t-ratio	p-value
Hired for permanent job	50.8%	53.3%	–	–	–
Likelihood of hiring for permanent job	3.33 (1.31)	3.42 (1.24)	–.07	–0.21	.831
Likelihood of hiring for summer job	3.67 (1.23)	3.79 (1.15)	–.10	–0.43	.671
Composite index of 13 interview questions ("A" items)	3.92 (.58)	3.93 (.57)	–.02	0.17	.863
Composite index of applicant qualities ("B" items)	3.86 (.76)	3.89 (.72)	–.04	–0.13	.901

youth got this answer right, as evidenced by the high scores for both groups on this item. Indeed, in our debriefing sessions with the HR interviewers, they indicated that few youth had trouble with this answer. So even though ASM2009 scored statistically higher on this item, the control youth did very well themselves. This item also did not correlate highly with HR ratings of whether they would hire youth, suggesting limited impact (see Table 2.3).

Similarly, the only item on which there was a statistically significant effect on the B scale was how well the young person had completed the job application. The completed job application was given to the interviewer at the start of the interview. Again, however, this item had the second lowest correlation of the B items with HR ratings of youth hirability. Moreover, ASM2009 did not spend any time on preparing youth for completing job applications, so it is difficult to think that this finding is very meaningful.

What Might Account for the Lack of Differences between ASM2009 and the Control Group?

One of the first places to look for an understanding of evaluation findings is the implementation of the target program. It is not unusual for there to be major problems in implementation that question the integrity of the intervention itself. However, our observations did not reveal any major problem with the integrity of the programs in the thirteen apprenticeships. All of the

TABLE 2.2 *Marketable job skills: Treatment-on-the-treated comparison*

	ASM2009 N = 135 M (SD)	Control N = 169 M (SD)	Effect size (g)	Treatment t-ratio	p-value
Hired for permanent job	56.3%	54.4%	–	–	–
Likelihood of hiring for permanent job	3.47 (1.26)	3.44 (1.26)	.02	1.08	.282
Likelihood of hiring for summer job	3.83 (1.16)	3.79 (1.15)	.04	1.23	.220
Composite index of 13 interview questions ("A" items)	4.01 (.52)	3.95 (.56)	.11	1.97	.049
Composite index of applicant qualities ("B" items)	3.97 (.71)	3.88 (.73)	.13	1.76	.079
1A – Why applied	3.68 (1.03)	3.52 (1.12)	.15	1.79	.075
2A – What experiences do you have	3.61 (1.32)	3.53 (1.27)	.06	1.44	.152
3A – Recent goal	3.65 (1.23)	3.75 (1.27)	-.08	0.48	.631
4A – Working with others	4.13 (1.03)	4.16 (1.06)	-.03	0.07	.947
5A – Complete a project by deadline	4.14 (1.08)	4.08 (1.12)	.05	0.84	.403
6A – Situation dealing with angry person	3.59 (1.40)	3.73 (1.28)	-.11	-1.22	.825
7A – Disagree with supervisor	4.63 (.70)	4.44 (.89)	.23	2.20	.029
8A – Stay late to cover shifts	4.53 (.81)	4.44 (.89)	.11	1.14	.256
9A – Special event conflict	4.48 (.95)	4.44 (.95)	.04	0.32	.753
10A – Trouble with photocopier	4.64 (.83)	4.49 (.89)	.17	1.52	.129
11A – How job contributes to future	3.84 (1.25)	3.79 (1.27)	.04	0.81	.418
12A – Questions about job	3.47 (1.67)	3.28 (1.63)	.12	1.37	.172
13A – What else about you	3.71 (.86)	3.63 (.93)	.09	1.12	.266

1B – Initial impression	3.57 (1.06)	3.52 (1.04)	.05	0.82	.414
2B – Appropriate dress and appearance	3.98 (.97)	3.73 (1.00)	.25	1.73	.085
3B – Eye contact	4.21 (.97)	4.02 (1.05)	.19	1.57	.118
4B – Positive attitude	4.01 (.97)	3.97 (1.04)	.04	1.05	.295
5B – Body language	4.30 (.86)	4.19 (.96)	.12	1.13	.259
6B – Confidence	3.83 (1.08)	3.83 (1.10)	<.01	0.45	.650
7B – Paid attention	4.44 (.80)	4.41 (.78)	.04	0.86	.393
8B – Communication	3.79 (1.07)	3.65 (1.12)	.13	1.89	.059
9B – Maturity	4.01 (1.10)	4.06 (1.13)	-.05	0.42	.677
10B – Application completion	3.84 (1.22)	3.63 (1.18)	.18	2.44	.015
11B – Prior experience	3.22 (1.14)	3.15 (1.29)	.06	1.28	.201
12B – Response to feedback	4.43 (.72)	4.42 (.74)	.01	0.84	.402

TABLE 2.3 *Permanent hiring rating and individual interview item correlations*

	Permanent hiring rating $r =$
"A" questions	.69**
1A – Why applied	.47**
2A – What experiences do you have	.48**
3A – Recent goal	.41**
4A – Working with others	.41**
5A – Complete a project by deadline	.34**
6A – Situation dealing with angry person	.42**
7A – Disagree with supervisor	.25**
8A – Stay late to cover shifts	.24**
9A – Special event conflict	.23**
10A – Trouble with photocopier	.21**
11A – How job contributes to future	.44**
12A – Questions about job	.19**
13A – What else about you	.39**
"B" questions	.86**
1B – Initial impression	.57**
2B – Appropriate dress and appearance	.34**
3B – Eye contact	.52**
4B – Positive attitude	.66**
5B – Body language	.58**
6B – Confidence	.68**
7B – Paid attention	.59**
8B – Communication	.76**
9B – Maturity	.82**
10B – Application completion	.51**
11B – Prior experience prepared student	.66**
12B – Response to feedback	.64**

* Correlation is significant at the 0.05 level (2-tailed).
** Correlation is significant at the 0.01 level (2-tailed).
N = 444–445.

programs were operated according to the ASM2009 model; in particular, there was a strong emphasis on developing skills in all of the apprenticeships. All of the instructors had relevant expertise and experience. There were no instances when apprenticeships did not meet for extended periods or did not obtain needed equipment within a reasonable period of time.[14]

Nevertheless, we were struck by two factors that could explain the lack of differences on the development of marketable job skills. We present an overview of the findings here. In Chapters 3 and 5, we explore these considerations in more detail, with additional data and analyses.

The first factor concerns program quality. All of the apprenticeships had been nominated for inclusion in the research by ASM2009 staff in the belief that they were among the best in ASM2009. In our observations, at least five of the apprenticeships were exemplary. In those apprenticeships, the apprenticeships produced interesting, original products and the instructors did a good job of creating a positive, effective culture. For example, students in the culinary apprenticeship focused intensely on producing food and food presentations of very high quality, and those in the Web design apprenticeship produced attractive websites for imaginary stores that sold products of personal interest to the apprentice who designed the site.

However, in our observations of the thirteen apprenticeships, three did not meet our expectations in terms of some important dimension of program quality. One of the instructors had such poor communication skills that the students were often confused or treated in a hostile manner. Another instructor had such weak expectations for quality that many of the student products resembled those that might be found in an elementary school arts-and-crafts program. A third instructor never learned the names of most of her students, was unfocused, and all but three youth eventually dropped out.[15]

It is difficult to imagine that youth in an apprenticeship in which the instructor had poor communication skills would find a positive role model for communicating job experiences, something that is essential in a job interview. Indeed, as can be seen in Table 2.3, HR ratings of the youth's overall communication skills had the second strongest correlation with hiring ($r = .76$) of any of the mock job items. It also stretches the imagination

---

[14] This is not to say that there were unimportant process differences among the ASM2009 apprenticeships. Some of these are presented and analyzed in the next chapter.

[15] If all but three youth dropped out of one apprenticeship, the young people who remained must have been unusual, and thus makes doubtful that the initial randomization into ASM2009 and control group was sustained. This is why methodologists are skeptical of results from treatment-on-the-treated analyses.

to think that producing poor quality work gives anyone an advantage in a job interview. Overall, thus, the quality of the apprenticeships varied more than expected on important variables.

The second factor that appears to explain the lack of statistically significant results concerns the failure of most ASM2009 instructors to talk about important soft skills that their youth were acquiring.[16] Although some instructors explicitly referred to how hard skills (technical skills required in a particular occupation) or soft skills (generic work skills useful in a wide variety of fields) obtained in the apprenticeship transferred to actual employment situations, most did not. The most frequent reference to transferability was a negative one, in which youth were scolded for their behavior and warned that, "You won't be able to get away with that on a real job!" Identification of positive soft skills that were being learned, and often further developed over the course of twenty weeks, were rare. There also were fewer instances than we expected in which marketable hard skills acquired in the apprenticeship were discussed in terms of actual employment opportunities that they could generate for youth. For example, in one otherwise excellent apprenticeship, focused on Web design, the only instance in which we observed a reference to the fact that youth could get paid for their design skills came during a presentation by a guest instructor. It therefore was not surprising when the HR interviewers, during debriefing sessions, informed us that many of the young people did not realize that they had marketable job skills (we focus on this factor in Chapter 5).

CONCLUSION

To test whether participation in ASM2009 results in marketable job skills, we collaborated with senior HR professionals to develop the first mock job interview for high school students. However, ASM2009 did not differ statistically from the control group on youth hiring, nor on A or B subscales, in the more methodologically rigorous, intent-to-treat analyses. The very few differences that emerged in the treatment-on-the-treated analyses were not that meaningful. Our initial explanation for the failure of ASM2009 to produce superior impacts revolves around variation in program quality

---

[16] For the importance of soft skills, see, for example, Casner-Lotto & Barrington (2006); Conrad (1999); Moss & Tilly (1996, 2001); Moss & Tilly (2001); Murnane & Levy (1996); Neumark (2007); Partnership for 21st Century Skills (2008); and Secretary's Commission on Achieving Necessary Skills (1992). These are sometimes referred to as generic skills, new basic skills, or noncognitive skills.

among ASM2009 apprenticeships and the lack of explicit verbal attention in apprenticeships to identifying skills that employers would value.

We explore these factors much more deeply in Chapters 3 and 5, adding additional data and more analyses. One of the benefits of our evaluation is that we obtained a considerable amount of qualitative data, using varied assessment procedures. We will also utilize a number of analytic frameworks to push our analyses. The results that we will subsequently report reveal how this kind of mixed-methods research can unravel why ASM2009 did not have a statistically significant impact. It will also point the way to needed improvements and, indeed, new programs that could be used to promote successful school to work transitions (Chapter 6). We cannot claim that we will have demonstrated causality in this additional research, as we could have with our impact analyses in the experimental design, but we will elaborate some very strong explanations and hypotheses that can contribute to the field.

3

A Comparison of the Strongest and the Weakest Apprenticeships

A prominent, large-scale program that garners considerable resources yet produces no statistically significant effect on one of its principal targets – marketable job skills – should concern policymakers, program administrators, employers, and researchers. As we search for effective ways to improve the labor market prospects for minority youth, it is prudent that scarce resources are allocated to program models that produce results. Although we did not find an overall effect of those thirteen After School Matters (ASM2009) apprenticeships on marketable job skills in comparison to the control group, that is not the end of the matter. It was clear from looking at the data that there was wide variation across apprenticeships in the relative performance of ASM2009 and control youth on the mock job interview. Some apprenticeships outperformed their control group, and some did worse. It could be that such differences arose merely by chance and were not substantively meaningful. But if important processes underlie those differences, pinpointing them might suggest critical improvements that could be targeted in program design that could then lead to better outcomes. Accordingly, in the next phase of our evaluation research, we sought to leverage this variation to address two questions: Are there identifying characteristics of the apprenticeship environment that distinguish the best- and worst-performing ASM2009 apprenticeships on the mock job interview? If present, do these salient characteristics provide possible explanations for apprenticeship-level differences in marketable job skills?

METHODOLOGICAL APPROACH

To maximize the likelihood of finding between-group differences, we used an extreme group design. We selected the two apprenticeships whose

This chapter is coauthored by Kendra P. Alexander.

TABLE 3.1 *Comparative mock job interview hire rates of study programs*

Program	Percent-hired apprenticeship (%)	Percent-hired control (%)	Difference
Best Hire:			
Youth View (print media)	79	32	+47
SongScape (music)	75	47	+28
Worst Hire:			
FUNdamentals (recreation)	27	53	−26
Tech Time (technology)	22	50	−28

participants were hired at the highest rate relative to controls (hereafter referred to as "best-hire" programs) and compared them to the two apprenticeships whose participants were hired at the lowest rates relative to controls (hereafter referred to as "worst-hire" programs) on the mock job interview.[1] The hiring variable we used was whether the youth would be hired for a permanent job, our most stringent hiring variable. The mock interview results of the four apprenticeships selected for this study, along with the results of their respective control groups, are presented in Table 3.1.

The ASM2009 apprenticeships examined in this phase of the research operated in three Chicago public high schools that serve predominantly low-income, minority student populations.[2] Let us now briefly describe the four apprenticeships (pseudonyms are used for all apprenticeship programs and individuals in this book.)

> *SongScape* (besthire). Students in SongScape form teams that compose and perform original songs, culminating in the production of a CD engineered in a professional music studio.

[1] The program with the absolute lowest comparative interview hire rates was omitted from the analysis owing to the extremely small number ($N = 3$) of students who participated in the mock job interview from that apprenticeship. We also excluded one of the best apprenticeships in terms of hiring rates as the coder (Kendra Alexander) had prior knowledge of this apprenticeship as being one of the top performers; this apprenticeship (Elite Eats) is discussed in the next chapter.

[2] Demographically, the four schools ranged from 96 percent to 99 percent African American and from 83 percent to 92 percent low-income. There was a marginally significant effect on age where best-hire apprentices ($M = 15.62$, $SD = 1.29$) were older than those in worst-hire programs ($M = 16.12$, $SD = 1.1$); $t (88) = 1.98$, $p = .051$. Chi-square tests showed the relationship between gender and best-hire or worst-hire status to be insignificant, $\chi^2 (1, N = 90) = 1.91$, $p = .17$.

Youth View (best hire). Youth View apprentices learn graphic design skills while developing and publishing a magazine issue targeted to an urban youth audience.

FUNdamentals (worst hire). This apprenticeship teaches the fundamental skills of three sports and how to lead activities for a child-centered recreational curriculum that was designed to be implemented in the forthcoming summer.

Tech Time (worst hire). In Tech Time, apprentices refurbish used computers. Tasks include testing hard drives, wiping memories, and installing operating systems and software. Students also learn help-desk support and networking basics.

Sixty-six sets of fieldnotes (representing approximately 200 hours of program observations) formed the corpus of data for this study. Weekly observations of each apprenticeship were made by members of our research staff over the course of a school year (ten weeks in the fall and ten weeks in the spring). It should be noted that we did not observe any of the formal afterschool activities in which members of the control group were engaged. Our focus is entirely on any differences between the best- and worst-hire ASM2009 apprenticeships.

In analyzing these data, we could have taken a deductive approach, developing and testing specific hypothesis about underlying process from the psychological, sociological, and economics literature that has highlighted various personal and interpersonal "soft skills."[3] These soft skills, such as initiative, perseverance, and leadership, are presumably valuable across a wide range of work fields, and thus appropriate when considering four very different apprenticeships (in contrast to "hard skills," such as computer repair, which are useful in a specific type of work). We also could have tested hypotheses derived from the literature on characteristics of effective youth programs, such as appropriate structure, positive social norms, and supportive relationships.[4] However, we were sensitive to the fact that little prior research had been done in this area and much needed to be learned. We did not want to circumscribe our inquiry prematurely, particularly given that we had collected an especially rich set of qualitative data. So we

---

[3] Almlund et al. (2011); Heckman & Rubinstein (2001); Heckman et al. (2006); Kuhn & Weinberger (2005); Lerman (2013); Lindqvist & Vestman (2011); Masten et al. (2010); Murnane & Levy (1996); Roberts et al. (2007).

[4] A particularly important publication in this area is the report by the National Research Council and Institute of Medicine committee on community-level programs for youth (Eccles & Gootman, 2002).

decided, instead, to take an inductive approach and explore from the bottom up what the data could tell us.

We used a grounded theory approach, which is often used in inductive qualitative research.[5] This involves multiple rounds of coding.[6] Initially, more fine-grained characteristics were coded regarding instructor and apprentice behavior (e.g., showing initiative, correcting), as well as the structure and functioning of the respective environments. After the initial round of coding, additional codes were added for a variety of off-task apprentice behaviors (e.g., horseplay, laying head on desk) and instructor responses. Attention then turned to identifying relationships between and consolidating codes. A second iteration of thematic coding was undertaken to identify those relationships. During this round of coding, unique patterns of interaction were noticed at three interpersonal levels: instructor-to-instructor, instructor-to-apprentice, and apprentice-go-apprentice. A third round of coding was undertaken to identify interactions at each of these levels. All coding was done blind to the relative performance of each apprenticeship on the mock job interview outcome to prevent any bias resulting from expectations related to "best hire" or "worst hire" status.

RESULTS

The iterative coding process led us to focus on teamwork and communication, as well as professional orientation, as the most salient overarching categories. Stark differences existed in these categories between the best-hire and worst-hire apprenticeships. Table 3.2 provides a summary of these differences.

Teamwork and Communication

As implemented, the two best-hire programs facilitated teamwork and communication between and among apprentices and instructors that promoted collegiality, collaboration, and reciprocity. In contrast, communications in the two worst-hire apprenticeships were often characterized by combative and unsupportive, superficial interactions. We present these differences in three domains: instructor-to-instructor, instructor-to-apprentice, and apprentice-to-apprentice.

---

[5] Strauss & Corbin (1994).
[6] Fieldnotes were analyzed using NVivo software.

TABLE 3.2 *Characteristics of apprenticeship work environments*

	Teamwork and communication	
	Best hire	Worst hire
Instructor to instructor	Collegial, cooperative	Combative, uncoordinated
Instructor to apprentice	Cooperative, nurturing	Authoritarian, distant
Apprentice to apprentice	Collaborative, supportive	Ad hoc, superficial
	Professional orientation	
	Best hire	Worst hire
Attendance and tardiness	Infrequent tardiness, moderate degree of absence	High attrition, frequent absence and tardiness
Orderliness and productivity	Order was maintained even with moderate distractions	Chaos was contagious
Initiative and self-direction	Self-directed and motivated	Waited for instructions and used idle time to socialize

Instructor-to-Instructor

With few exceptions, instructors in Youth View and SongScape (the two best-hire apprenticeships) modeled effective teamwork and communication skills to their apprentices. In both of these apprenticeships, there was a clear hierarchy between the instructors, where Eric and Leslie (SongScape) and Shannon and Corey (Youth View) operated as lead and assistant instructor, respectively. Although there was a chain of command, both instructor teams shared responsibility and showed respect for each other's skills and opinions. During one recording session in the music studio, a colleague teasingly commented to Eric on the leadership role that Leslie has assumed for the day, to which Eric responded casually "I told her on the first day we had equal say. She can fire whoever she wants, do whatever she wants …". At times, Eric vetoed Leslie's ideas, but when he did so, he generally explained his reasoning, and although Leslie's face sometimes appeared to register disappointment in Eric's decisions, she did not sulk or otherwise undermine the working relationship. It is notable that Eric and Leslie had extensive prior professional experience working together outside of ASM2009.

In YouthView, Shannon and Corey established a laid-back cooperative environment. Most sessions included examples of them sharing easy small talk and doing small favors for each other, such as retrieving materials from each other's car. They regularly helped each other by equitably reallocating the workload if it became unevenly distributed. Shannon and Corey also had professional differences of opinion, but they resolved their differences constructively. At times they would talk their differences out with each other and reach a compromise. In other instances, they would bring in third parties, usually the apprentices, to provide a new perspective and allow this "tie-breaker's" opinion to resolve the disagreement.

In contrast, the most disturbing instructor-to-instructor dynamics occurred in FUNdamentals, one of the two worst-hire apprenticeships. Mr. Wagner, a veteran ASM2009 instructor, led the FUNdamentals program for the entire twenty weeks. All of the sports apprenticeships were designed so that three co-instructors were rotated in to assist the lead instructor with specific sports. Unlike Eric and Leslie, who came into the SongScape apprenticeship with an existing working relationship, Mr. Wagner and Ashley, his first co-instructor, met each other on the first day of the FUNdamentals apprenticeship. There were problems in the working relationship between Mr. Wagner and Ashley from the beginning, with evidence of a power struggle noted in the first observed session.

Ashley openly expressed disdain for her co-instructor to the researcher, something that never occurred during the observations in the best-hire apprenticeships. There appeared to be a disconnect between Ashley's understanding of her role and how she felt she was being treated. Instead of addressing her concerns to Mr. Wagner, she first complained to the researcher taking fieldnotes. Throughout her tenure, Ashley regularly communicated frustrations with Mr. Wagner through her body language, facial expressions, silent sulking, sighs and other audible noises to convey her displeasure, and by discussing her feelings with the researcher.

Mr. Wagner also disclosed his frustrations with Ashley to the researcher. He regularly ignored Ashley's input, gave apprentices instructions that conflicted with those given by Ashley, and interrupted her when she spoke. In the seventh week, their relationship deteriorated to the point of a shouting match in front of the apprentices. Ashley stormed out of the gym after the exchange and never returned to the apprenticeship after this session. The serious communication problems between these two instructors were evident to the students, one of whom commented in retrospect, "They never meshed." At no time did the researcher observe constructive conversations take place between Mr. Wagner and Ashley to discuss their differences.

In Tech Time, the other worst-hire apprenticeship, an offhand comment intended to be facetious provided a fairly accurate foreshadowing of the relationship between Mr. Evans and Mr. O'Leary, the co-instructors of this apprenticeship. Mr. Evans noted, "We don't work as much of a team, I just shout a lot, and he knows about computers." A joint lecture by the instructors illustrates this point:

> (Mr. O'Leary) is … delivering concepts and detailed information in a way that I can see the students are unable to grasp completely. Some are frowning and looking confused. During Mr. O'Leary's presentation, Mr. Evans interrupts and takes over in order to make it simpler for the students. He … tries to simplify all of what Mr. O'Leary was trying to say, but essentially does so by telling the kids they will be told what they need to do and not to worry about it.

Although Tech Time instructors presented a united front and refrained from open conflict, their lack of coordination and on-the-fly decision making is very different from the planned and organized communications of the best-hire instructors. The lack of coordination hampered the operations of the program. Instruction was haphazard and ad hoc, with regular blocks of idle time where the apprentices waited for direction from either instructor. In addition, it was clear at times that the instructors had not coordinated their lessons, leading to confusion and disengagement among the apprentices.[7]

Instructor-to-Apprentice

Instructors also differed in the patterns of interaction they maintained with apprentices. In the best-hire programs, instructors and apprentices worked cooperatively, and instructors formed nurturing and caring relationships with the apprentices. In contrast, the instructors in worst-hire programs were comparatively distant, and often authoritarian.

---

[7] We emphasize that we are considering these apprenticeships in relation to the hiring outcome on the mock job interview. The two apprenticeships that are defined by their scores on that variable as worst hire need not have scored poorly on other outcomes. For example, the Tech Time apprentices learned important hard skills and did well on a measure of self-efficacy. FUNdamentals apprentices had very positive views of Mr. Wagner that they expressed to us in focus groups at the end of the second semester. These factors suggest why ASM2009 supervisors might have considered them high-quality apprenticeships despite the evidence reported in this chapter. Furthermore, these qualitative data reflect the performance of the apprenticeships at the time of our assessment and do not necessarily reflect how these programs might have functioned prior to our involvement or subsequently.

In both of the best-hire programs, instructors made an effort to begin each session with an activity or gesture to find out what was going on in the students' lives. At the beginning of almost all of the SongScape sessions, Eric and Leslie invited students to share "throw-ins" or "throw-aways" – positive or negative aspects of their day. Examples of common throw-ins included high grades earned, gifts received, and progress with their music in the apprenticeship. Throw-aways often included mentions of disciplinary actions, conflicts, or personal loss. This activity provided an immediate opportunity for apprentices to share personally meaningful feelings and experiences as well as to listen respectfully to the thoughts and feelings of others. It also communicated from the get-go that there was a plan and order to each session that apprentices needed to follow. Similarly, Shannon began many Youth View sessions by asking students about the details of their day or weekend or by following up on issues and concerns that students had mentioned in previous sessions. Practicing this type of easy banter and give–and–take could help students gain comfort with the type of informal collegiality that can promote a positive work environment.

For the most part, the instructor-to-apprentice interactions in the best-hire programs were characterized by mutual respect, with the instructors occasionally referring to and treating the apprentices as colleagues. When correction or admonishment was required, Eric regularly utilized silence to redirect off-task behavior in SongScape apprentices. Owing to the rapport he had established with the youth, his signature statement, "I'll wait," followed by silence, almost always resulted in the cessation of off-task behavior. Likewise, Shannon usually only had to point out to Youth View apprentices that their inappropriate conduct was "disrespectful" and they would almost always respond and adjust their behavior accordingly.

Regarding conversations related to the work itself, best-hire apprentices engaged in more substantive conversations with instructors that involved critical thinking and exchange of ideas. Shannon posed questions to Youth View apprentices such as "Why do you think that this design was designed the way it was?" She would prod further, challenging students to identify how they might approach the design differently, including a justification for their reasoning.

Looking across instructor–youth behaviors in best-hire apprenticeships, this interactional style corresponds to a type of parenting that social scientists have labeled "authoritative." Widely documented in research as the gold standard, including for African Americans, authoritative parenting involves warmth, responsiveness, and open communications, while also setting clear limits and having high expectations.[8] The value of this approach has also been documented in the school setting.[9] Authoritative mentoring in these apprenticeships seems just as valuable as is authoritative parenting at home. We will return to the topic of authoritative instructor mentoring in the next chapter.

In contrast, the primary communication style in worst-hire programs was oriented toward instructors providing instructions and apprentices following them. Youth in the FUNdamentals apprenticeship did not respond well to the authoritarian leadership style of Ashley, the co-instructor who left the program after a blow-up with Mr. Wagner. In the work session prior to Mr. Wagner and Ashley's altercation, Ashley lost her temper with a group of girls in the apprenticeship, openly berating and shaming them in front of the larger group.

Similar negative outcomes occurred in Tech Time. Mr. Evans made several ill-conceived attempts to connect with apprentices; his speech often had a sarcastic and demeaning edge to it. When reviewing self-appraisals that the apprentices completed about their computer skills, he loudly remarked "Oh sure! I can't believe you put that! I never saw you do that." or "Uh uh uh uh, you don't do things on time. It took you two days to do this simple assignment. Why would I pay you $27 an hour?" He also regularly peppered his instructions with comments such as "Shut up!", "Sit Down!", "Did I say you could do that?", or "What's the matter with you?"

Apprentice-to-Apprentice
In the best-hire programs, apprentices worked together to accomplish goals and were largely supportive of one another's work, providing constructive feedback and encouragement. In the second apprenticeship session that we observed, Eric explicitly set out his expectations for interactions between the SongScape apprentices, "Anything we talk about in here is constructive criticism.... When you're criticizing, you can be like, 'I have a suggestion. I think on the second verse you can try this.' Then you said your piece and you aired it out." For the most part, SongScape apprentices adhered to this norm. Not only did they respectfully critique each other's work, but they also provided feedback and support regarding workplace relations. In the

---

[8] Baumrind (1991); Larzelere, Morris, & Harrist (2012); Maccoby & Martin (1983); Mandara (2006).

[9] Wentzel (2002) found that similar dimensions in the relationship between middle school teachers and students were associated with student motivation, social behavior, and achievement. Walker (2008) reports similar results; though see Dever & Karabenick (2011) for more nuanced findings.

following episode, Janelle, an apprentice who had been named to a leadership position among her SongScape peers, encourages another apprentice, Amir, who expressed disappointment with the group assignment that he received:

> She tells Amir in an animated tone, "Lamont and I had never said even one word to each other" before they had to work together, and the only thing she knew about him was that he was always making condescending remarks about "homos" [Janelle is a lesbian.] She asked pointedly, "How do you think I felt, going in there?" Amir nods slowly, and Janelle concludes by telling him bluntly to "Suck it up."

Janelle's recommendation that Amir "suck it up" could be inferred negatively. We talked to the research observer about this incident to get a better appreciation of Amir's response to Janelle's last statement. The observer indicated that Amir responded affirmatively and that he did so because he interpreted her statement as a well-intentioned motivational tool. This speaks to the mutual respect that apprentices developed for each other in the best-hire apprenticeships. Among urban youth, the slightest perception of disrespect can often result in escalation of negative emotions and violence.[10] Thus it is notable that in both best-hire programs, in which some apprentices were conferred meaningful authority over their peers, this arrangement was received with compliance and cooperation.

In both best-hire programs, creative collaboration was the main work style utilized and peer-to-peer critique was a core function of the process. Early in the program, SongScape apprentices were assigned to groups of four and worked collaboratively on all aspects of composing and performing their song. During the second half of the Youth View apprenticeship, Shannon and Corey organized teams of four around functions that included an illustrator, a page designer, a photographer, and an art director. Each participant was expected to contribute a meaningful and unique component to the layout.

Apprentices in worst-hire programs did not engage in teamwork to the extent of those in the best-hire programs. FUNdamentals apprentices often worked in dyads as partners, were assigned to groups for drill practice and skill development, or were split into teams when playing games involving the sports that were part of the programs' emphasis. Similarly, TechTime apprentices often performed parallel tasks in an assembly-line style

---

[10] Anderson (1999), Chaiken (1998), Hirsch (2005). See Deutsch (2008) for an especially insightful analysis of the reciprocity of respect in youth programs.

formation. In both of these apprenticeships, substantive interactions were limited. These apprentices did not engage in the back-and-forth exchange of ideas and negotiation of responsibilities that those in the best-hire programs experienced.

Although there were instances of positive apprentice-to-apprentice interactions in the worst-hire programs, these apprenticeships were more likely to have examples of participants in antagonistic relations with each other. FUNdamentals apprentices regularly ignored direct instructions to work collaboratively or did so begrudgingly. Here, a prompt for two FUNdamentals apprentices to communicate with each other verbally during partner drills is ignored:

> *While Jesse and Monique pass [the ball], Mr. Wagner actively provides input, "Control, control, talk to your partners. You talk to each other all day. Talk to your partners." Neither Jesse nor Monique talk to each other or respond to Mr. Wagner's comments. They continue to pass until Mr. Wagner moves on to another group, at which point, both Jesse and Monique sit on their balls near the wall without saying a word to each other.*

FUNdamentals apprentices regularly socialized with each other during breaks and idle time during the work session. However, this camaraderie did not translate into communicating effectively on apprenticeship-related tasks.

To summarize the main differences between communications in the best- and worst-hire programs, the best-hire programs were characterized by effective teamwork and respectful, reciprocal communications on all three levels: instructor-to-instructor, instructor-to-apprentice, and apprentice-to-apprentice. Apprentices in best-hire programs were treated by their instructors as individuals with valid ideas and opinions to share. When problem behaviors arose, the apprentices were generally treated with respect and their behavior calmly redirected. They were also provided ample opportunities to share personal concerns, as well as those related to the apprenticeship. Best-hire programs utilized both small group and large group activities, in which apprentices engaged in brainstorming, idea sharing, and giving and receiving constructive criticism. In contrast, apprentices in worst-hire programs were often taunted, berated, yelled at, and shown other forms of disrespect by their instructors. In worst-hire apprenticeships, directions were given by instructors and followed by apprentices, generally without soliciting the input of the youth participants. The worst-hire programs had far fewer examples of rich communication and were plagued by discord in the relationships among program participants at all levels.

Professional Orientation

The other main set of differences between best- and worst-hire apprenticeships was with respect to the professional orientation of the apprenticeship. There were important difference in norms regarding attendance and tardiness, orderliness and productivity, and initiative and self-direction. Best-hire programs generally established expectations and norms around professionalism that more closely mirror those that would be found in a mainstream work environment. Worst-hire programs were significantly more lax in the communication and enforcement of such norms (see Table 3.2).

Attendance and Tardiness

Two core expectations of any employer are that employees will attend work reliably and that they will arrive at work punctually. Attendance and punctuality had to be addressed in all four apprenticeships. On most of the observed days, the best-hire apprenticeships had attendance rates of 75 percent or higher. By the middle of the worst-hire apprenticeships, it was not uncommon for more than 50 percent of apprentices to be absent on any given day.

When a Youth View apprentice was absent due to suspension from school, Shannon emphasized to the group that such absences are considered unexcused. In another session, she explained that apprentices should schedule doctor and other necessary appointments during nonapprenticeship hours when possible. In contrast, instructors in the worst-hire apprenticeships rarely addressed late arrivals with a reprimand or any other form of disciplinary action. They appeared to be excused for other school-related obligations, including tutoring, sports team practices, and detention. These apprentices would regularly leave or return mid-session, but their reduced participation did not affect their pay because apprentices were paid based on the number of days they attended and not the number of hours. Therefore, a person in a worst-hire apprenticeship who attended for one hour received the same pay as an apprentice who attended for the full three hours.

Orderliness and Productivity

In mainstream work environments there is often a low buzz associated with the rhythm of the work setting. Some offices permit music at low levels, people stop at cubicles to chat with each other, and they congregate in lounge areas, providing the backdrop for the term "water cooler talk." In a functional office, all of this coincidental activity does not prevent work from getting done.

In Youth View, with few exceptions, off-task behavior that rose to a level of disruption could be redirected appropriately with one comment from the instructor. SongScape apprentices often needed multiple requests to settle down, but were generally cooperative.

A core order existed in best-hire apprenticeships where a moderate amount of noise and nonwork focused activity usually did not lead to a complete breakdown of order. To foster productivity, instructors in best-hire programs were more intentional and consistent in the communication and enforcement of expectations regarding the maintenance of attention to task, limiting horseplay, and ensuring that work was actually getting done. This is what one would expect of a consistently authoritative style of workplace mentoring.

In contrast, apprentices in the FUNdamentals program regularly defied direct requests to perform work-related tasks or to refrain from behaving in certain ways. Apprentices in leadership roles with Tech Time regularly played cards during work time. Other apprentices in Tech Time regularly surfed the Web, watched YouTube videos, or communicated on Facebook during work time, with minimal or no effort to conceal their activities. Instructors in the worst-hire programs largely ignored these behaviors, and when addressed there were generally no consequences for the apprentices disregard for authority as seen in this example from Tech Time.

> At one point [Mr. Evans] says loudly, "Mr. O'Leary is speaking. Why aren't you listening?" Things quiet down, but it is not apparent that the students are all paying attention. Two have their heads down (Mr. Evans goes over and taps this student on the shoulder), two are still whispering, one is playing a video game of some sort.

Unlike the regular efforts to establish an environment that promoted orderliness and productivity that occurred in the best-hire programs, attempts to do so in the worst-hire programs were haphazard and ineffective.

There were some behaviors present in both best-hire and worst-hire programs that detracted from the work environment. In all four apprenticeships, there were instances of multiple side conversations being conducted when an instructor was talking, as well as "play fighting," talking or texting on cell phones, aimlessly milling around the room, and surfing the Internet. Instructors in the worst-hire programs ignored much of this disruptive behavior, and by doing so may have contributed to the lack of the core order that instead characterized the best-hire programs. Although they were not always successful, instructors in the best-hire programs made more consistent and early attempts to redirect problem behaviors before they escalated to a type of contagion that permeated the entire work environment.

Initiative and Self-Direction

In an employment setting, supervisors rarely address each task that a worker is expected to perform individually. Employees are expected to possess some degree of initiative and self-direction. Apprentices in both best-hire programs often moved between tasks without being told, resulting in a seamlessness to the operations of these programs. In the example that follows, SongScape apprentices minimize idle time while the technical staff prepare the equipment in the recording studio.

> As Devon and Tony work with the equipment, Stacy, Jordan, and Keith rehearse their song. They talk quietly as they review the song's structure, and I can just barely overhear them discussing the order and length of the various parts.

Apprentices in the worst-hire programs had a significant amount of idle time and almost always had to wait for further instructions to move from one task to another. In FUNdamentals, early-arriving apprentices shot hoops or gathered in groups to socialize on the bleachers. They were never observed practicing previously learned drills to perfect skills related to the apprenticeship. Likewise, Tech Time apprentices regularly used any idle time to play cards or engage in other forms of socializing. This kind of behavior is not surprising given the lack of clear expectations, minimal response to norm violations, and fractured communication among instructors in these apprenticeships. Like the differences in teamwork and communications, these contrasts in professional orientation represent defining characteristics of the best-hire and worst-hire programs.

LINKING APPRENTICESHIP DIFFERENCES TO MOCK JOB INTERVIEW PERFORMANCE

We have seen that there were important differences in teamwork and communication, and in professionalism, between the two best-hire and the two worst-hire apprenticeships. We believe that these apprenticeship-level differences are likely to account for different hiring rates in the mock job interview.

In the best-hire apprenticeships, apprentices regularly engaged in meaningful discussions with their instructors and peers regarding the apprenticeship work. This gave the apprentices practice in explaining their views, elaborating ideas, justifying stances, asking and answering questions about their work, and giving and responding to feedback. Our HR interviewers told us that these are important skills that need to be displayed in employment interviews.

The best-hire apprentices were also exposed to the norms of real workplaces. They had to work and comport themselves according to high standards. They became familiar with what is expected at any real job. This understanding – and maturity – is one of the qualities that interviewers are looking for in young workers. Recall that interviewers' ratings of maturity were the best predictor of hiring on the mock job interview (see Chapter 2).

The collegial atmosphere in the best-hire apprenticeships fostered the development of an ease and comfort when talking to adults. This is an important skill for an interview setting, where the nonverbal interchange is very important. Interviewers, moreover, are likely to interpret this facility as another sign of maturity.

The HR interviewers placed a high priority on being able to function well as a member of a work team. This is consistent with findings from a national study of HR leaders in corporate America that emphasized the importance of teamwork as a top skill looking forward to the future.[11] Regular team interactions provided best-hire apprentices with experiences that mimic relational styles common in the modern work world.

Young people in the worst-hire apprenticeships were not exposed to these types of work environments. They did not typically engage in meaningful discussions about their work with instructors or peers; they were not regularly exposed to the norms of real workplaces; their communications with instructors were not such as would lead to ease and comfort in relating to adults; and, though they did sometimes work together, the parallel tasks that they performed did not require the same degree of teamwork. They thus had fewer positive, work-relevant experiences to discuss with HR interviewers, and less experience with give-and-take communications about work with adults.[12]

---

[11] Casner-Lotto & Barrington (2006).

[12] There were additional factors that could have worsened the performance of youth in worst-hire apprenticeships. Because instructors in those programs often modeled inappropriate behavior, such modeling might lead participants to adopt an "if they can do it, so can I" attitude where they devalue the importance of self-presentation and cultivating positive work relationships. Furthermore, by regularly ignoring inappropriate conduct in apprentices, instructors might have caused the participants to view their conduct as acceptable or "good enough" and adjusted their personal standards accordingly. Finally, apprentices in worst-hire settings may have adopted an apathetic stance in the interview that mirrored their lack of engagement in the apprenticeship. Interviewers are not likely

IMPLICATIONS

We have seen that differences between best-hire and worst-hire apprentice-ships are meaningfully related to difference in teamwork, communication, and professionalism. These domains tap important social and emotional skills whose importance has been highlighted in numerous reports by business study groups and by social scientists.[13] The social environments, or culture, of the best-hire apprenticeships also correspond well to features of effective youth settings identified by the National Research Council (NRC).[14] Specifically, the NRC included the following among features of positive developmental settings: appropriate structure, supportive relation-ships, opportunities to belong, positive social norms, support for efficacy and mattering, and opportunities for skill building. These qualities seem to be well represented among the best-hire apprenticeships and less well so among the worst-hire apprenticeships.

If we wanted to summarize, in an integrative manner, the various quali-ties of the best-hire apprenticeships, we could say that these settings helped youth to appreciate and adapt to the culture of the contemporary work-place. The culture of the best-hire settings served as a reasonable analogue to what would be required of youth at real work settings. The settings, and the mentoring provided by their adult leaders, helped young people to understand and demonstrate competence in the roles they would ulti-mately be required to fulfill.

This approach to understanding the value of best-hire apprenticeships is consistent with psychologist Barbara Rogoff's cultural perspective on human development. Rogoff views development as the "transformation of participation in cultural activities."[15] These data suggest that a primary task of youth programs designed to increase marketable work skills is to engage youth in and socialize them to an environment in which young people assume adult roles in work-like settings.

Stephen Hamilton, in a frequently cited study of German appren-ticeships for young people, reached similar conclusions.[16] He found that

to hire anyone who doesn't appear to be motivated and enthusiastic (Moss & Tilly, 1996, 2001; Neckerman & Kirschenman, 1991).

[13] For example, Casner-Lotto & Barrington (2006); Heckman et al. (2006); Kuhn & Weinberger (2005); Lindqvist & Vestman (2011); Partnership for 21st Century Skills (2008); Secretary's Commission on Achieving Necessary Skills (1991).

[14] National Research Council and Institute of Medicine (2002).

[15] Rogoff (2003), p. 37.

[16] Hamilton (1990).

employers emphasized *Arbeitstugende*, or worker virtues, as a major criterion in hiring. These worker virtues correspond reasonably well to what we have referred to as soft skills and included qualities such as diligence, responsibility, receptivity to supervision, willingness to work hard, reliability, precision, and punctuality. Hamilton believed that "strengthening worker virtues is the most beneficial effect attributable to youth work experience." A major function served by German apprenticeships was in helping youth to develop what "they need to know and be able to do in any job."[17] As we noted in Chapter 1, the German apprenticeship system is considered the gold standard for youth workforce development, so finding similar processes underlying best-hire ASM2009 apprenticeships suggests that we are highlighting a critical ingredient for developing marketable job skills.

Implications for Hiring and Training

If the overarching value of the best-hire ASM2009 settings resides in immersing youth in a work-like culture and developing the soft skills needed to function effectively in work settings, then it must be said that the criteria that ASM2009 used to hire instructors did not align with that objective.[18] ASM2009 leadership stated that they hired instructors based on their substantive expertise in a line of work, rather than on their youthwork skills. Another way of stating this is to say that instructors were hired based on their hard skills and not their soft skills. ASM2009 leaders asserted that youth felt that many of their school teachers lack such expertise and they did not want to replicate that situation in ASM2009. Having technical expertise would give instructors needed credibility with youth.

ASM2009 believed that they could then train instructors in youthwork skills, or what we might consider soft skills of special importance to working with youth. Our observations, however, are that several of the ASM2009 instructors we studied were lacking in the social and organizational skills needed to make their apprenticeships effective, despite having received ASM2009 training. And, recall, these apprenticeships were considered by ASM2009 to be among their best.

The quality of ASM2009 instructor training was a topic that we discussed each year with the organization's leadership. We did so, in part, because they

[17] The first quote is from p. 24 and the second is from p. 86 (Hamilton, 1990). Lerman (2013) discussed this issue outside of the German context.

[18] Hirsch, Deutsch, and DuBois (2011) emphasized how organizational variables, such as hiring and human resource (capital) development, can influence the effectiveness of after-school programs.

repeatedly told us how they had revamped their training and made it much more effective. During the second year of our study, we informally asked the instructors about ASM2009 training. None of them had much good to say about the training ASM2009 had provided. Thus, not only did ASM2009 not hire for soft skills, but the quality of youthwork training they provided was of questionable effectiveness.

Given the need for improved hiring and training, the importance of ongoing formative evaluation of instructor training cannot be overstated. It is important to examine hiring criteria, initial instructor skill level and attitude toward teaching marketable job skills, the skillfulness of the trainers, learning of concepts, and how well exposure to training translates into behavior in the apprenticeship. Our findings also suggest that it would be useful to modify the hiring criteria, so that soft skills are considered as well as hard skills. If youth soft skills are to be enhanced, it would be helpful to have instructors who are strong in that area.

Implications for Null Findings in ASM2009 Evaluation

Findings from this extreme-group analysis of ASM2009 apprenticeships provide a portal from which to consider the lack of statistically significant differences in marketable job skills between ASM2009 and the control group. *Qualitative* findings from this chapter suggest that there was wide variation in the focus and effectiveness of the apprenticeships in creating adult-like work environments. There also appeared to be wide variation in the focus on soft skill development.

These qualitative differences are consistent with findings from *quantitative* analyses that were conducted on possible differences between ASM2009 and the control group on how youth perceived the social climate of their respective program. ASM youth rated their apprenticeship experience, whereas youth in the control group rated their experience in their most time-intensive extracurricular activity. For these analyses, we made use of social climate scales developed by psychologist Rudolf Moos. We combined items into a single scale that tapped Involvement (from the Work Environment Scale), or the extent to which youth put a great deal of effort into their projects; Task Orientation (Work Environment Scale), which measured the focus on getting work done; Cohesion (from the Group Environment Scale), which assessed belongingness and group spirit; and Leader Support (Group Environment Scale), which tapped the supportiveness of the adult leader.[19] There were no significant

---

[19] The total scale, which combined items across those four subscales, had adequate reliability ($\alpha = .86$). Further information on these scales can be obtained from Moos (1974).

differences between the social climate of the apprenticeships versus the control group extracurricular settings.[20] It should also be noted that higher social climate scale scores were significantly associated with a greater likelihood of being hiring ($r = .13$, $p < .05$), as measured by HR ratings on the mock job interview. Thus, although the social climate measure is not an exact reflection of the setting characteristics identified in our qualitative analyses, they are similar enough and, moreover, are statistically linked to mock hiring rates, suggesting their importance to employment. The correlations do not prove causality, but they provide empirical support to the argument that has been made in this chapter.

The combination of qualitative and quantitative findings suggests that ASM2009 apprenticeships were not sufficiently different from control group settings on variables crucial to the development of marketable job skills. Even among ASM2009's better apprenticeships – which were the focus of this evaluation – the failure to consistently build apprenticeships with stronger, positive cultures, and that encouraged soft skill acquisition, diminished the ability of ASM2009 youth to develop marketable job skills superior to what they might develop in an alternative program.

Social Policy Implications

A further implication of these findings is with respect to social policy. If we consider the culture of these four programs, the best-hire programs represent the kind of culture that most youth programs hope to achieve, regardless of the youth outcomes they pursue. This overlap suggests that youth in well-run after-school programs may gain the kinds of soft skills that were found in the best-hire ASM2009 apprenticeships, skills that led professional HR interviewers to say that they would hire those youth if they had a real job opening. On a policy level, this suggests an important rationale or justification for youth development programs: they can help youth to develop marketable job skills. Positive youth development programs have often had difficulty gaining policy traction because they don't have the kind of "problem" rationale that can lead to public funding. Most youth development programs are not primarily designed to treat or prevent youth problem behaviors, such as drug or alcohol abuse, teen pregnancy, criminal behavior,

---

[20] The ratings for the ASM group ($M = 3.94$, $SD = .55$) were trivially higher than for the control group ($M = 3.87$, $SD = .54$), the difference being nonsignificant statistically ($F = 0.81$, $p = .369$).

school dropout, and so on. But, in this analysis, we found that they may well help youth develop marketable job skills, and workforce development is an important national objective whose value is much clearer to policymakers. This is an important argument for the field. It reframes the linkage between youth development programs and meaningful society outcomes.

SUMMARY

Most program evaluations would have stopped analyses with the quantitative findings reported in the prior chapter. Instead, in this chapter we used the extensive qualitative data obtained as part of our mixed-method inquiry to see if there were meaningful differences between best-hire and worst-hire ASM2009 programs. Our analyses revealed important differences with respect to teamwork, communications, and professionalism. We then argued that those underlying differences could well explain differences in the hiring rates between youth in the two best and two worst apprenticeships. Finally, we considered the implications of those findings for staff hiring and training, and for social policy.

In the next chapter, we continue our evaluation of ASM2009 by using qualitative data to examine two of the better apprenticeships as determined by hiring rates on the mock job interview. One of these is SongScape, which we examined in this chapter. The purpose of the next chapter is to consider which of those two good programs, which have very different program designs, serves as the best model to replicate. We believe that there are important differences in how well each is likely to be implemented at scale, even though both were effective.

4

Which Apprenticeship Has the Best
Model for Scaling Up?

Overall, youth in ASM2009 apprenticeships did not demonstrate more marketable job skills than their peers in alternative after-school programs and activities. Yet in the previous chapter we saw that some apprenticeships outperformed their control group and that the way in which those apprenticeships functioned could meaningfully explain their better performance on the mock job interview. At this point, we want to elaborate our analysis of some of ASM2009's most effective apprenticeships and explore whether they are positioned to serve as models for programs that seek to integrate positive youth development with workforce development.

Two ASM2009 programs stand out as exemplary and worthy of consideration. We observed these two apprenticeships during our last year of data collection and had our eye on them from early on. During the first semester, it became apparent from our field observations that these two were generating unusual levels of student engagement, the activities were quite skill-focused, and they were oriented toward producing recognizable products that would be presented toward a broad community. The mock job data justified our enthusiasm, as both emerged as among the strongest ASM2009 apprenticeships, producing much better hiring rates than their respective control groups.[1] In short, these apprenticeships strongly subscribed to the ASM2009 guiding framework and produced excellent outcomes. Despite important generic similarities, they were nevertheless designed and implemented in very different ways. Not only that, but the different approaches corresponded to very strong social science theories, from different disciplines, that enjoy considerable support.

[1] Hedge's $g = .45$ for SongScape and $.57$ for Elite Eats.

This chapter is coauthored by Megan A. Mekinda.

One of these apprenticeships is SongScape, which was introduced in the last chapter. SongScape taught basic skills in lyric and music composition, album production, and live performance. Over the course of the year, youth collaborated to write original songs, record them on a group album (the main focus of the apprenticeship), and choreograph and perform the pieces for an audience of family and friends at an end-of-semester showcase. In our view, this apprenticeship corresponded well to the authoritative model of how adults can best lead youth, first studied in relation to parenting, and more recently utilized in other settings, such as schools. This model has considerable support in the developmental science literature, especially among psychologists. As part of what we shall term the authoritative mentoring model, the instructors also made explicit attempts to socialize youth to professional roles in songwriting and production, and an emphasis on socialization to roles has a strong history in the social sciences, especially in sociology.

The second apprenticeship was Elite Eats, which focused on developing basic skills in menu planning, food preparation, and food presentation. The apprenticeship was ultimately responsible for planning and delivering several meals, including a gala event hosted by ASM2009 at a landmark Chicago theatre. The most distinctive feature of the apprenticeship was a series of competitive cook-offs; apprentices were divided into two teams and each prepared and presented a complete meal to a panel of outside judges. The winning team was determined through judges' scores on predetermined criteria. The losing team, alas, was tasked with clean-up. The competition model, of course, finds its academic home in economics and is a core value in our capitalist economic system.

We will proceed by first presenting specific features of each model, drawing on our fieldnotes and interviews, and emphasizing the apprenticeship's fit to its corresponding theoretical model. We will then consider how well each model might be implemented by others. In this way, we seek to mine the findings for promising future directions. If we were in charge of a program and wished to consider whether to implement either of these two approaches, we might well review our own existing programs and their adult leaders to consider how well the approach would work for them. What we as researchers can do is to draw on our extensive data on the other eleven ASM2009 apprenticeships, including our personal familiarity with them, to analyze the feasibility of implementing the authoritative mentoring and team competition models. We will see that this approach yields a number of insights that may be broadly applicable to the wider universe of youth development programs that seek to promote marketable job skills.

Qualitative data analyses were completed in two distinct phases. The purpose of the first phase was to delineate core components of the SongScape and Elite Eats models, based primarily on analysis of the 600 pages of fieldnotes documenting 36 observations of the two apprenticeships. The purpose of the second phase, the anticipatory implementation analysis, was to determine the extent to which core components of authoritative mentorship and organized competition could be realized within the 11 remaining apprenticeships, based primarily on 1,800 pages of fieldnotes documenting 170 observations. Both phases involved a process of active and iterative reading of the data, informed by a set of guiding questions (e.g., how do instructors establish and maintain each model? Could youth's work be evaluated by outside judges who do not have specialized knowledge or expertise?). A series of analytic memos were written that described key patterns in the data and our evolving assertions related to the main research questions. Through a series of case analysis meetings, we discussed the content of the analytic memos, debated alternative interpretations, and considered implications for ongoing data analysis. A more extensive discussion of the qualitative methodology is available elsewhere.[2]

THE SONGSCAPE MODEL

The concept of an authoritative relationship is well established in the literature on parenting and its effects on child development. For nearly a half century, the field has been profoundly influenced by the work of psychologist Diana Baumrind, who promoted a typology of parenting styles based on two dimensions.[3] *Demandingness* reflects the extent to which parents assert their authority, set limits on their children's behavior, and communicate high expectations. *Responsiveness* reflects the extent to which parents are affectionate and loving with their children, respect their children's psychological autonomy, and express acceptance and support. An authoritative parent is high on *both* dimensions, and thus "antithetical both to the permissive prototype characterized by few rules or demands and to the authoritarian prototype characterized by coercive and functionally superfluous control."[4]

Decades of research attest to the widespread benefits of authoritative parenting. These include greater social and cognitive competence, emotional

---

[2] Mekinda (2015).
[3] Baumrind (1966, 1991, 2013).
[4] Baumrind (2013), p. 13

and psychological health, healthy behavior (e.g., less smoking), and academic achievement among children of authoritative parents as compared to those from authoritarian or permissive homes.[5] Research beyond the field of parenting indicates the benefit of authoritative practices outside the home. For instance, teaching styles that reflect high levels of both demandingness and responsiveness are linked to gains in students' academic interest, motivation, and achievement.[6]

Like authoritative parents, SongScape instructors set a high bar for youth performance and behavior, and they were insistent that youth strive to meet these expectations. They critiqued youth's work openly, persistently enough at times to elicit tears from a frustrated apprentice. Instructors were also swift and firm in addressing apprentices' behavioral digressions, for example, the exchange of childish insults or refusal to collaborate. True to ASM2009's commitment to work readiness, SongScape instructors rationalized these demands by making explicit the direct and immediate professional significance of youth's apprenticeship experiences. For instance, they refused to tolerate conflict among apprentices to prevent youth from "burning bridges" and sabotaging potentially lucrative contacts, "especially this early in the business." They made mandatory a weekend photo shoot for the album cover, set strict guidelines for youth's dress and styling, and insisted that youth rehearse their smiles and postures beforehand, all for the sake of public relations. Regarding the publicity photos, Eric, the lead instructor, asserts "This is how people tell who you are.... If you don't have a face, you don't exist [in the music business]. I'm dead serious."

In the excerpt that follows, Eric outlines in no uncertain terms his expectation that youth do well in an upcoming audition for the year-end ASM2009 showcase, which, he explains, could be the jumpstart to youth's professional careers:

Eric addresses the apprentices in a firm tone, "I'm warning you now. The showcase audition is very competitive." He explains that the group will be competing with 150 other programs, the members of which "will have full costumes. They will be prepared. On point." ... Eric continues, "My past groups have gone in and killed it. Killed it.... I mean for you to do the same," but he stresses that the youth must work hard. He says the experience is important because it makes SongScape "look good," but adds

---

[5] Baumrind (2013); Berge et al. (2010); Castrucci & Gerlach (2006); Darling (1999); Steinberg (2001); Steinberg, Elmem, & Mounts (1989).

[6] Dever & Karabenick (2011); Gregory & Weinstein (2004); Hughes (2002); Scarlett, Ponte, & Singh (2009); Walker (2008); Wentzel (2002).

that it's especially important for the apprentices themselves because, "It's exposure on a mainstream stage for you all." He quickly lists a few famous artists who have performed in the Chicago Theater, such as Beyoncé, and tells students that the audience will be full of "a zillion and one rich people who can drop a dime for your demo tape. It's an excellent opportunity for you all. Think about that." He concludes by reminding the students once again that for the rest of the semester they need to be really focused: "Have fun, but we got work to do."

Eric rationalizes his insistence on hard work and quality performance by highlighting the potential payoff for youth's careers via exposure to wealthy sponsors. To further legitimate his demands, he relates youth's experience to that of professionals in the field, in this case, to some of the industry's megastars.

Perhaps the most powerful connection between the apprenticeship and the professional music industry were regular visits to a professional recording studio, distinguishing SongScape as the only apprenticeship in the evaluation routinely to expose participants to an adult work environment. Youth had an opportunity to see and experience their instructors' workplace and also to interact with other professionals in the field. These included sound engineers, the studio manager, and various artists who also used the facilities. Instructors welcomed apprentices to the space with enthusiasm and invited them to take advantage of the opportunities it had to offer. Yet, they were blunt in their insistence that the opportunity came with the obligation of hard work and professional behavior. This meant arriving to each recording session prepared and well rehearsed. It also meant accepting stern critique of one's performance and advice for how to improve. In the following excerpt, Eric reminds the youth of their role in the studio:

Eric tells the apprentices that on the way home from the studio, "Janelle [apprentice] said on the bus, 'It was cool being in the studio because what was in my head actually came out.'" He [Eric] stresses in an enthusiastic tone that this is exactly how all students should feel when they get into the studio, that they should be able to communicate exactly what they're thinking to the engineer "instead of standing there like, 'Uh duh,' or 'I dunno!'" Eric says this last phrase in a mocking and sarcastic tone. He also tells the students that Jordan [sound engineer] was impressed with Janelle "because she knew exactly what she wanted" and was easy to work with. Jordan also asked when Janelle would be back. Eric asserts, "What they said about her is what I want to hear about everybody." He concludes, "I'm not expecting your first song to be on the radio ... I'm expecting mess-ups. The first time you ride a bike, you do fail," but that at the same time, "this is

a professional game, y'all" and the youth need to be as prepared as possible
if they're going to make progress.

Again, Eric is clear about his expectations for youth performance and
behavior, and he identifies Janelle, an apprentice, as an attainable model. He
relays feedback from the sound engineer, a professional in the field, to justify these demands. Eric acknowledges that the youth are novices and likely
to mess up, but this does not preclude the fact that they are involved in a
"professional game" and, beginner status notwithstanding, must act like it.

As these examples illustrate, instructors' expectations were elevated and
explicit, and framed in a way to entice youth contemplating their role in the
professional world. By highlighting the professional significance of apprenticeship experiences, instructors *urged youth to identify as already active*
contributors to the field as opposed to merely aspiring artists. Thus, they
created a context in which youth could interpret high demands as requirements for professional success as opposed to mere demonstrations of the
instructors' authority. In a workforce development context, the high expectations or demandingness of the authoritative style is expressed via the
strong press toward socialization in an occupational role.

There was an additional factor to make such demands more palat-
able: instructors' abundant warmth and support, the complementary component of authoritative mentoring.[7] Instructors displayed their fondness for
apprentices in ways typical of skilled youth workers: Eric generally through
goodhearted teasing and dry humor and Leslie, the co-instructor, through
earnest conversation and physical affection. They made themselves readily
accessible both during and outside of programming hours, prominently dis-
playing personal cell phone numbers and email addresses on the classroom
white board. Over the course of the year, instructors were observed advis-
ing or consoling youth over a range of personal issues such as a peer conflict, poor report card, or tragic loss. Furthermore, they made a concerted
effort to establish warmth and supportiveness as a general norm within the
apprenticeship. On one occasion, for example, when she felt there was "a lot
of negativity in this room," Leslie initiated a group exercise in which youth
sat in a circle and took turns saying "something nice, something positive
about the person to your right." Leslie elaborated on what youth had to
say with her own sincere and enthusiastic compliments. A youth initially
reluctant to join the activity was encouraged by a peer to "Come sit down

---

[7] Steinberg (2001).

with your family, guy!" evidence of instructors' successful establishment of a caring program environment.

As with their framing of demands, instructors also tailored their supportiveness to the work-like setting of the apprenticeship, focusing praise and encouragement on youth's developing skills as songwriters and performers. Throughout a typical session, they delivered personalized instruction and feedback, perhaps coaxing a shy youth to sing a verse aloud, complimenting another on a well crafted lyric, and coaching a third on breathing techniques for vocal performance. They urged apprentices to speak out when they were confused, stuck, or dissatisfied, and commended them for speaking up when they had ideas. A testament to instructors' mastery of authoritative practices, examples of their work-related support were generally inextricable from demonstrations of high demands, as in the following excerpt:

> After hearing his group assignment, Lamont [apprentice] groans loudly, pulls his hat low over his eyes, and throws his weight back in his chair. He sits for a few seconds with his hands over his face, then leans forward again in his chair and shakes his head. Leslie asks what's wrong and he complains that he is not happy about his new group because he and Michael "Just don't get along. We don't get along, man." He is also unhappy about working with Kayla because, "Kayla, she just gonna try to take over the whole thing," and he's concerned about the "new kid" because, "I don't even know what he does" (e.g., sing, rap). Eric, Leslie, and Janelle [senior apprentice] listen patiently as Lamont talks. After he finishes, Eric is silent for a moment. Then, he tells Lamont that he's sorry Lamont doesn't like his group, but he must find a way to make it work. Eric prods, "You gonna turn down a contract for a million dollars because you hate the person you'd have to record with?" Eric talks rapidly for about two minutes, emphasizing that "in the real world" Lamont will have to work with people he doesn't like. He provides a few examples from his own experience, such as a teacher he "loathes," but, he says, "I put a smile on my face and make it work." He adds with a snort, "I think you might even make friends with some of these people if you let yourself" and says he thinks Lamont can teach the new kid a few things about rapping.

In this exchange, Eric is firm but empathetic. He listens patiently to Lamont's concerns, issues a directive, and justifies it by relating it to the professional world. He shares a personal anecdote to relate to the youth, and finally, he flatters Lamont by emphasizing how his talents will contribute to the group's progress. The exchange illustrates precisely the type of warm and supportive action, attuned to youth's vulnerabilities and individual needs, described by Baumrind with regard to authoritative parents.[8] Here, Eric has skillfully adapted the practice to support youth's professional development within the apprenticeship.

For their part, SongScape youth recognized instructors' abilities to complement high demands with warmth and support, and they respected and admired them for it. During an end-of-year focus group, apprentices described Eric and Leslie as friends, partners, even family, but insisted that "with Eric and Leslie you still know your boundaries," and "They keep it real, let you know what's up" with frank and honest feedback. One apprentice describes her relationship: "Even though they are advisors, bosses, they're my bosses, but I still see them as my friends. They're like my family.... They brought something to the table that no one else has tried to do: Constructive criticism." Overall, the instructors' mentoring style garnered great trust and fondness among the youth. As one apprentice enthused, "I love them. *Love* them.... They're patient, fun to be around, great authoritative figures, *outstanding* musicians.... Terrific role models."

Distinctive Benefits for Job Interviews

The SongScape youth are strongly socialized to see themselves as workers, as already having entered an occupation or profession. This will facilitate viewing their apprenticeship experiences as work relevant and make it easier to draw on them during (mock) job interviews. Not all ASM2009 youth view themselves as workers and thus do not count many of their experiences as work relevant (see Chapters 5 and 6).

Youth experiences in SongScape emphasized commitment and high quality standards, characteristics that are likely to positively influence prospective employers. Apprentices repeatedly rehearsed a particular song or verse – even a single phrase – until it reflected their instructors' quality demands; youth stayed late in the studio to meet strict production deadlines; and they expended considerable effort to resolve conflict within their groups to prevent personal issues from undermining project goals.

Moreover, thinking of themselves as young workers is likely to impress the HR interviewers as reflecting maturity, as going beyond the more child-like student role, as thinking independently and with a work orientation. Speaking eagerly about their confidence gains during a post-program focus group, apprentices described themselves as "bolder" as a result of their participation in SongScape which they claimed influenced their behavior

---

[8] Baumrind (2013).

and attitude both within and beyond the apprenticeship context. As one apprentice shared, "I believe in myself. This [the apprenticeship] helped me to know that I *do* believe in myself." A second explained, "I'm more confident that I can achieve.... It [the apprenticeship] made me realize that there are certain things I have to do and that I can get them done.... It's made me more mature, like a grown-up person." Maturity and confidence, as rated by the interviewers, are strong predictors of mock hiring (see Chapter 2).

Eric constantly provides a rationale for different activities. Given this constant exposure, youth in SongScape are likely to incorporate these rationales into their way of thinking. In the job interview, HR professionals are intent to uncover how someone thinks, how they evaluate situations, how they decide to act in a certain manner. SongScape apprentices are used to discussing these issues with Eric and likely will more easily draw upon these understandings when asked during the job interview than would youth from most other apprenticeships.

More general features of the authoritative approach will also be useful. The youth are likely to have found comfort in interacting with adults, and may have a higher level of trust that the interviewer is interested in discovering a young person's potential rather than shortcomings.

ELITE EATS

Our focus with respect to Elite Eats is on the competitive cook-offs specifically, rather than on a comprehensive analysis of the apprenticeship experience. The cook-offs were the distinctive element of this apprenticeship.

The research team's observations of cook-off sessions were truly noteworthy with regard to the intensity and persistence of youth engagement. To foster engagement is a common challenge among after-school programs, including the apprenticeships in our study. This was not a problem on cook-off days. Youth entered the classroom and began work immediately with minimal socializing, downtime, or time wasted for the duration of the session. They wanted to get to work:

> It was as if they had taken a nap a few hours before and had come in totally refreshed and eager to work. Nobody had their head down, nobody looked bored, they were just sort of eager beavers, cheerful, light on their feet, and wanting to do their stuff.

Youth maintained a high level of intensity and engagement throughout the 2.5 hours allotted for the cooking, as described in the following fieldnote:

I now move over to Team Two in order to see what they are working on. Emma is making a homemade ranch dressing for their broccoli dish. Julia and Mindy are making brownies. Jesse is working on chopping the pork and seasoning it. Isabel is working on making a hash brown casserole with corn flakes. The students are working very quickly, but calmly. Claudia has already started to clean up around her team's tables and picks up used bowls and materials to take to the sink area. Others on her team follow Claudia's lead and start clearing off dishes and utensils that have already been used.... Ellen [instructor] comes back into the room and yells out, "What time is it? Keep track of your time. It's now 3:41PM. You've got one hour and fifty minutes!" The students continue working. They do not seem startled or rushed by her reminder, but continue to work steadily and at a determined pace.

In this excerpt, the six youth named are working diligently on five different tasks. Those without a task assist where needed, in this case by cleaning the workspace. Consistent with researchers' observations throughout cook-off sessions, the level of participation appears to be equal among team members; all youth contribute, as opposed to the team being "carried" by one or a few highly motivated members. Furthermore, youth maintain a sharp focus on their goal – to prepare and display their dishes before the 5:30PM buzzer – and they are managing their time well.

In addition to staying on-task and focused during cook-offs, youth were also highly committed to product quality. Apprentices' attention to detail and persistent efforts to improve their work are illustrated in the following excerpt, which describes one team's process of designing the display table for their prepared menu items:

[4:30 PM] Team Two is concerned that their table does not look as good as Team One's table. They are vocal about their concern and say things like "Their table is so good," and "Our table is so tacky." ... [Alejandra's] team tries to work with the Mardi Gras thematic colors and materials, and they keep rearranging their set up in order to try to create something they like.

[4:45 PM] B asks Ellen if she thinks their table is ugly. Ellen laughs and says, "I can't say. I have to be impartial." Alejandra then looks at me and says, "It is, isn't it?" I shake my head and smile.... A few moments later Ellen calls out for Alejandra from her office. I hear Alejandra yell, "Whoo hooo! We're going to win now!" She runs out of Ellen's office with a box. Alejandra brings it back to the table and the girls from her team crowd around. Alejandra starts taking out strands of lights and other festive materials. The team starts to work together to add on to their already bright and festive-looking table.

[5:00 PM] The rest of the room is quietly working. Team Two is still fussing over the decorations and setting of their table where they will be presenting their dishes.

As the time markers indicate, the team members worked on their table for approximately forty-five minutes, determined to create a display on par with the opposing team. They persisted with this task at their own insistence to meet their own high standards, rather than at the suggestion of the instructor. Indeed, instructors' expectations for youth performance were modest. Yet, under these competitive conditions, youth were driven to produce consistently high-quality work. Their plated dishes resembled what one might reasonably expect to find at a restaurant such as T.G.I. Friday's or the Olive Garden.[9] The careful arrangement of various food items and the addition of garnishes and other decorative touches were testament to the youth's keen attention to detail.

Youth competed under clearly defined parameters. The menu guidelines and scoring rubric (see Figure 4.1) outlined specific tasks to be completed and the criteria on which they would be evaluated. Clear and specific rules, procedures, and criteria for winning are key characteristics of "appropriate competition," competition most likely to lead to constructive experiences and outcomes.[10] Such parameters allow youth to focus energy on optimal performance as opposed to questions of fairness or integrity. They also undermine opportunities to dispute winners and losers, which can lead to feelings of bitterness and resentment. Judges for the cook-offs included, on different occasions, school guards, available teachers (nonculinary), members of our research staff, and someone with a professional culinary background. Notably, the Elite Eats instructors were never part of the judging panel; they always maintained neutrality and served as technical consultants to both teams.

Youth enjoyed receiving feedback from the judges on their performance and, not surprisingly, they especially enjoyed being on the winning team. In the following instance, the youth in Elite Eats are favorably compared to those in an advanced culinary apprenticeship:

One of the judges who had previously tasted something from the advanced apprenticeship class said that this was at least as good if not better than what the advanced apprenticeship had done. The kids roared when they

---

[9] These are affordable, full-service restaurants that are part of national chains.
[10] Johnson & Johnson (1989, 2005); Stanne et al. (1999).

	Team 1	Team 2
Entrée: Pork		
Taste	_____	_____
Presentation	_____	_____
Appetizer		
Taste	_____	_____
Potato dish		
Taste	_____	_____
Cake dessert		
Taste	_____	_____
Presentation	_____	_____
Overall presentation	_____	_____
TOTAL:	_____	_____

FIGURE 4.1. Judges' score sheet for intergroup competition within Elite Eats. Ratings on a scale from 1 to 5 (5 = best) for each menu component listed.

> heard that because naturally they [advanced apprentices] are the big guys
> and to say that you are doing just as good a job and maybe better really
> stroked them a lot, and they were very appreciative ...

When the scoring rubrics for the cook-off were totaled across judges, the winner was announced and "the team that had won let out a yelp as if they were at a sporting event and their team had just won, they were screaming. And the other team, though clearly disappointed, were good sports about it." The principal investigator of the research (Hirsch) also observed this cook-off and lauded the youth for their intense engagement and consistent hard work, highly effective teamwork, commitment to quality, and group self-regulation. He considered it to be the single best ASM2009 apprenticeship session that he had observed – and better than all of the others by a considerable margin.[11]

---

[11] The instructors were not informed in advance that the principal investigator would be observing that day. The first note and the last two notes reported in this section were taken from transcriptions of Hirsch's remarks to his research team at their weekly meeting following this cook-off.

Distinctive Benefits for Job Interviews

The interteam competition drives a search for quality and improvement. It elicits maximum effort. Because competitions were between groups, and because tasks were differentiated, youth had to employ advanced collaboration skills. The menu guidelines and scoring rubrics gave youth practice in organizing resources, identifying and executing appropriate and feasible plans to accomplish a given goal, and demonstrating creative problem solving while adhering to constraints. Youth had to be efficient, meet a deadline, and manage stress and pressure. Competitive cook-offs also offered youth the positive experience of applying their skills in a challenging but enjoyable context, the type of experience that should leave a very positive impression on youth about the nature of adult work. All of this provided a wealth of experience that apprentices could draw on that would be likely to impress HR professionals.

Interaction with the judges could benefit youth as well. As apprentices described their dishes to judges, they experimented with how to sell a product, endeavoring to promote their work in ways both informative and pleasing. They were also subjected to judges' immediate and frank reactions to the taste and quality of their food. Salesmanship and receptiveness to feedback are themselves valuable job-related skills. Beyond this, youth's engagement with the judges was in some ways analogous to a job interview. In both cases, youth were put in the position of communicating with unknown adults, promoting themselves and their accomplishments, and submitting to face-to-face evaluation. Thus, the experience of outside judges provided valuable preparation for the interview experience.

Comparing the efforts of one's group to the competition can itself be a valued trait. One youth who interviewed for the mock position with Chicago Cool Clothes told the interviewer that he would be interested in going to competing clothing stores to study their displays and merchandising, bringing back information on competitors that could help Chicago Cool Clothes improve their sales. This youth suggestion made a very positive impression on the HR interviewer.

Finally, we might imagine that accounts of what the youth had learned from the cook-offs would be vivid and have a certain genuineness. The excitement and insights were not gained from an instructor or a book and there should be less doubt than there might be otherwise that the youth were merely parroting lines that they had been taught to tell. The HR interviewers had a particular aversion to anything that seemed like it might be a canned script to be delivered in a job interview.

ANTICIPATORY IMPLEMENTATION ANALYSIS

Delineation of effective program models is only a preliminary step in the scale-up process. The prudent subsequent stage is analysis of the models' feasibility across program settings.[12] Often, barriers to a model's implementation are uncovered and addressed ad hoc during the actual implementation attempt, undermining effectiveness and compromising valuable time and resources.[13] Implementation is a complex, multifaceted process often overlooked in studies of program effectiveness.[14] Existing research on youth programs suggests that implementation problems are both widespread and consequential.[15] In one meta-analysis, for example, poorly implemented programs yielded effects averaging just one-third to one-half the size of those from well-implemented programs.[16]

In this section of the chapter, we consider how successfully each of the models is likely to be implemented, using the remaining eleven ASM2009 apprenticeships as our research sample. Data comprised nearly 1,800 pages of fieldnotes documenting 170 observations across the 11 apprenticeships, which included reports of numerous conversations with instructors and occasional ones with their ASM2009 supervisors. We also analyzed the individual case studies, which contained researchers' summary assessments of key aspects of each site such as daily program routines, the nature of instructor–youth interactions, and patterns of youth engagement in program activities. We emphasize how likely each component of the two models is likely to be implemented with fidelity (i.e., as intended) and skill. Thus, we considered not only whether youth leaders were likely to take certain actions, but also the quality of the efforts they were likely to make.

Authoritative Mentoring

The good news is that instructors in four of the eleven apprenticeships were already practicing authoritative mentoring to some extent. Those instructors displayed high levels of both demandingness and responsiveness. One might imagine that in these instances some additional training could be

---

[12] Adelman & Taylor (2003); Fixsen et al. (2005).

[13] Fixsen et al (2005).

[14] Durlak (1998); Fixsen et al (2005). See Kelly & Perkins (2012) for recent work on implementation in educational settings.

[15] Durlak & DuPre (2008); Elias (1997); Gottfredson et al. (1997); Gottfredson, Gottfredson, & Skroban (1998); Hirsch (2005); Schorr (1989).

[16] Durlak & DuPre (2008).

provided to more fully flesh out the model as practiced in SongScape, particularly with respect to positive role socialization. The instructors' existing practices provide a strong foundation to build upon, and it seems likely that the amount of additional training the instructors would need to implement the model more fully would be manageable.

On the other hand, we anticipated serious challenges to successful implementation of the authoritative mentoring model in nearly two-thirds of the apprenticeships in the evaluation. Authoritative practices were inconsistent with important elements of how those instructors operated their programs. Authoritative mentoring is a complex concept, involving multiple skills, some of which will intuitively strike some instructors as inconsistent or contrary to their beliefs about how to run an apprenticeship. Training therefore would need to target a range of skills and attitudes, with no guarantee of successful adaption and implementation. The skills – and difficulties – reside in five domains:

- High demandingness
- Presenting the job relevance of apprenticeship experiences
- Poor communication skills
- Warmth
- Training requirements and costs

Upholding high *demands* for work behavior proved challenging for most instructors. Rules generally relaxed over the course of the year as instructors and youth became more familiar with each other and comfortable with the work of the apprenticeship. At times some instructors struggled to abide by their own rules, habitually arriving late or missing time owing to scheduling conflicts, personal problems, or health issues. Ultimately, fewer than a third of study apprenticeships maintained high demands for basic work behavior throughout the year.

Moreover, some instructors were simply uncomfortable enforcing strict rules, concerned that demandingness would undermine the casual atmosphere they desired or sour apprentices' experience in the program. These instructors prioritized fun and enjoyment, or they hoped to create an environment clearly separate from youth's grueling and rule-riddled school day. For example, one instructor worried that requiring youth to sit through three hours of work after a full day of classes was unreasonable. By the second semester, he dedicated large portions of each session to "free time," during which most youth elected to play video games.

Other instructors would need to be educated on the difference between authoritative and authoritarian forms of demandingness. Both are power assertive, but power in the authoritative sense is what Baumrind terms confrontive: reasoned, negotiable, outcome-oriented, and intended to regulate behavior. In contrast, power in the authoritarian sense is coercive: arbitrary, peremptory, domineering, and intended to mark status.[17] Based on these distinctions, instructors in three apprenticeships easily classified as authoritarian. For example, one instructor presented his expectations in the following manner: "You will be graded on getting from here to the [classroom] in an orderly way. You must line up. You must go with your supervisor and not leave your group. Everything you do from now on will be under a microscope, and you will be graded on everything.... I don't want anyone in this program who can't behave, so you can just leave if you don't want to do what I tell you."

In terms of another aspect of the SongScape model, many instructors did not *discuss apprenticeship experiences in terms of their job relevance.* Nearly all instructors told us that they believed in the value of their apprenticeship as a context for the development of marketable job skills. In practice, however, instructors made only occasional references to the professional significance of youth's experience, and these were almost universally negative or punitive in nature. Most commonly, instructors' efforts to relate youth's experiences to the professional world took the form of admonishment for behaviors that youth wouldn't "get away with" in a "real job." The following excerpt provides an illustration of this:

> *"Part of your responsibility in this job is to get up and do the assignments. I know this is hard for some people, but it is your responsibility to complete these tasks. This does not depend on your notion, gumption, ability or desire.... If this was a job in an office, where you have to do filing, answering the phones, and typing, you can't just decide one day that you aren't going to do filing, or you aren't going to answer the phone. There is no picking and choosing. You would be fired."*

By contrast, SongScape instructors most often capitalized on opportunities to relate youth's experiences to the professional world in positive ways, identifying and nurturing behaviors and attitudes required for success on the job and career advancement rather than harping on those to avoid punishment. There is a meaningful distinction between SongScape instructors' inclination toward positive framing of apprenticeship experiences, which encouraged youth's identities as professionals, and other instructors' negative orientation, which appealed more to their own authority.

---

[17] Baumrind (2012, 2013).

SongScape instructors had excellent *communication skills*, consistently providing youth with a thoughtful rationale for desired behaviors and quality standards. However, poor communication skills plagued instructors in at least a quarter of study apprenticeships. In these cases, well-intentioned efforts to provide instruction, feedback, or guidance were often inconsistent, confused, or only tangentially related to the immediate work of the youth. Several examples of poor instructor communication skills were provided in Chapter 3.

Warmth, or supportiveness, is an important element of the authoritative mentoring model. In six of the eleven apprenticeships, instructors consistently regarded youth with respect and care. Similar to SongScape instructors, they expressed interest in youth's personal well-being while nurturing skill development through encouragement, praise, and individualized feedback. These instructors were judged capable of implementing the supportiveness component of authoritative mentorship without training and ongoing supervision.

However, this leaves five apprenticeships – nearly half of the sample – in which instructors' relationships with youth lacked the warmth and support requisite for the model. In some cases, instructors remained aloof, engaging youth only as much as required for basic program functioning or as allowed by an overbearing co-instructor. In extreme cases, instructors displayed aggressive and even hostile behaviors toward youth, asserting their authority through screams, threats, and insults. Within these five apprenticeships, the research team documented instances of conflict, avoidance, frustration, and resentment between instructors and youth. We also witnessed patterns of petty yet heated arguments (often instigated by the instructors themselves), public shaming of youth, and the failure of two instructors – after weeks of program activities – to learn apprentices' names.

This is a rather daunting set of challenges for *training* and supervision. If you were in charge of a program, perhaps of modest size, whose instructors already exemplified much of the authoritative mentoring approach, such as four of the eleven apprenticeships in our sample, then the training strikes us as doable. However, if several staff persons are more like those in the other two-thirds of our sample, you would have to seriously question whether it is worth attempting to train them in this model. A good number of skills would need to be taught, many of which would be difficult. It would be necessary to challenge some fundamental staff beliefs and attitudes. Some staff would actively resist change in this direction. In addition, several of the ASM2009 instructors had well-formed personalities that we had seen were highly resistant to change. In addition to initial workshops, ongoing training and supervision – by those who were experienced and competent to serve in that capacity – would be essential. All of this would be costly, and there would be the real possibility that training would prove ineffective or would be sabotaged by trainees. Authoritative mentoring is a great model for workforce development in a youth development context, but it may well be too difficult to implement in many circumstances.

If the authoritative mentoring model is to be adapted, and if the skills and attitudes required of instructors cannot entirely be learned, then it needs to be considered whether at least part of the requisite skill set should be part of the hiring criteria. As Fixsen and colleagues conclude from their frequently cited, comprehensive review of the implementation literature, "Beyond academic qualifications or experience factors, certain practitioner characteristics are difficult to teach in training sessions so must be part of the selection criteria."[18] Some experimentation is likely to be necessary to identify the hiring profile that makes most sense for the multiple goals of these programs.

Organized Group Competition

We believe that organized group competition would be much easier to implement successfully than authoritative mentoring. The skills required of the instructors are fewer and less complex and the required training would be less extensive and less costly. In our detailed review of the qualitative data from the eleven remaining apprenticeships, we concluded that core components of the competition model could be readily implemented in approximately two-thirds of the apprenticeships with little change to existing structure and routines. Specifically, both of the co-authors of this chapter believe that this could occur in seven apprenticeships; we could not reach a consensus regarding an eighth apprenticeship.[19] This is in contrast to the authoritative mentoring model, where we anticipated serious difficulties in two-thirds of the sample.

---

[18] Fixsen et al (2005), p. 28.

[19] Regarding the one instance in which consensus could not be reached, one of the chapter coauthors believed, based on the fieldnotes, that one instructor would be philosophically opposed to implementing the group competition model, deeming it incompatible with his existing practices; the other author believed that the instructor was persuadable. We considered the first view, based as it was on actual instructor comments, to be the more conservative interpretation and use that when we coded for compatibility with existing practices. There was no disagreement regarding the coding of that apprenticeship on the other variables.

There are several factors that enhance the feasibility of adopting the organized group competition model:

- Compatibility with existing practices
- Ease of developing scoring rubric
- Impact on youth motivation, engagement, and quality of work

In addition to Elite Eats, there were a number of apprenticeships where *youth routinely collaborated in groups* and teammates took responsibility for unique roles and tasks. In a few other apprenticeships, independent projects could be restructured as collaborative with no obvious detriment to youth's experience or opportunities to learn. Projects in these seven programs required a repertoire of hard skills and also elements of taste, style, and creativity, which suggest natural parameters for competition and that could be evaluated by judges without expertise in the field.

The following excerpt provides one illustration. Here, an instructor from an arts-based apprenticeship describes guidelines for youth's next group project, an animated public service announcement about domestic violence:

> Yevette [instructor] explains that each group's film should have three characters and a new set.... Most of the film will be silent; however, at the end one character will talk. Yevette acknowledges, "This is when things can get a little tedious, but this is also when it starts to look like a real film." Each animation will comprise 60 pictures, as with past projects, but apprentices will also be required to add 12 "talking" pictures. To do so, they must make 6 mouths for their character. Yevette writes "a, e, i, o, u," on the board with spaces in between. She explains, "One mouth for each vowel. Can anyone guess what the other mouth is?" A couple of youth correctly guess, "Closed." Yevette tells apprentices to look at a group member as they say the vowels [so they know what shape each mouth should be].... Finally, apprentices are also required to craft two sets of eyes: one open and one shut. "You are using google [googly] eyes, so you will have to make [eye] lids out of clay."

In this case, youth completed the project in teams, with individual teammates taking responsibility for the crafting of each character figure, the design and creation of the set, and the staging and photographing of each frame for the animation. The structure of the task satisfied a number of the criteria for competitive group competition: collaboration in teams, differentiated tasks, specification of work that is to be completed, and application of cumulative skills that had been learned.

	Team 1	Team 2
Characters (3)		
Appearance	_____	_____
Animation: body movement	_____	_____
Animation: speech	_____	_____
Set		
Appearance	_____	_____
Artistic qualities		
Style	_____	_____
Creativity	_____	_____
Content		
Clarity of message	_____	_____
Compellingness of message	_____	_____
TOTAL:	_____	_____

FIGURE 4.2. Possible judges' score sheet for intergroup competition within an arts-based apprenticeship. Ratings on a scale from 1 to 5 (5 = best) for each component.

Youth's work in this apprenticeship could be readily adapted to a competition between teams to produce the best film (or film scene). Their activities could readily be translated into a *scoring rubric* that would enable judges to rate fulfillment of basic criteria (the presence of three characters and a set), technical skill level (the quality of animation, particularly the realistic appearance of speech), artistic qualities (style and creativity), and overall impact of the film (the compellingness of the message pertaining to domestic violence). We created a sample of such a rubric, modeled after the rubric for an Elite Eats cook-off, that appears in Figure 4.2.

An apprenticeship that focused on designing a mock website for a store selling products of the student's choice (e.g., athletic shoes, cosmetics, cars) provides a second illustration of how core components of the organized competition model could be implemented in various programs. Work in this apprenticeship was generally independent; yet, the occasional use of teamwork suggests no obvious drawbacks, and it could provide a welcome change to standard procedures. Individual teammates could take responsibility for the design of secondary pages to be linked to the main webpage, the drafting of content, and the selection and customization of desired graphics. Again, key aspects of youth's work convert readily to a competition rubric. In this excerpt, the researcher recounts an instructor's description of a "good" webpage five weeks into the apprenticeship:

> *During the course of the class, I ask Paul [instructor] what a good page would look like when completed. Paul says that it all depends on the kids. For now, he is prescribing certain visual aspects to their pages, such as a pop-up message of introduction when users enter the site, at least one video component, and audio on at least one page. But, after apprentices learn the basics, they can go back and tailor their sites specifically to the businesses they want to market. Right now, the good sites will simply be the ones that can execute the technical tasks he gives to them. Paul also adds that this will change once they learn how to tailor their graphics and learn Photoshop to make custom images. With custom graphics, those who put more effort and time into their pages will have more impressive end products.*

The presence of a pop-up message and video and audio components constitute basic criteria, and the proper functioning of each reflects technical skill. Judges could also rate the creativity and appeal of the overall design, as well as aspects of their experience as users of the site, such as navigability (see Figure 4.3 for a sample rubric that we created based on the Elite Eats model). Furthermore, the instructor's comments highlight an additional quality of work across apprenticeships relevant to the model's implementation: the possibility for competitions to evolve throughout the year as youth's skill set develops, as was the case in Elite Eats. In this apprenticeship, more weight could be given to the sites' graphics and artistic qualities as apprentices' skills in these areas progressed.

Although Elite Eats was the only apprenticeship to feature organized group competition as a central component of program activities, across the remaining sites we observed isolated instances (often impromptu) in which youth competed: for example, a "quiz show" to review coding information in the Web design apprenticeship, a race to network a series of computers in another apprenticeship, and a contest to produce the best faux commercial in an arts program. Without exception, youth embraced these opportunities with enthusiasm, often demonstrating a *noticeable surge in engagement and performance quality* in comparison to their behavior during routine apprenticeship activities.

The following example illustrates the impact of competition on youth behavior in FUNdamentals, the sports program presented in Chapter 3, when male and female apprentices challenged each other to a "dance-off" while practicing routines that could be taught to groups of young children:

	Website 1	Website 2
Pop-up message		
Functionality	_____	_____
Content	_____	_____
Video component		
Functionality	_____	_____
Content	_____	_____
Audio component		
Functionality	_____	_____
Artistic qualities		
Design	_____	_____
Creativity	_____	_____
Navigability	_____	_____
TOTAL:	_____	_____

FIGURE 4.3. Possible judges' score sheet for intergroup competition within a technology-based apprenticeship. Ratings on a scale from 1 to 5 (5 = best) for each component.

> *The boys begin the dance. In the final move, in which they are supposed to jump and turn 90 degrees, they all turn 180 degrees. As they turn, several boys yell, "Oooo!" and I hear one holler "What now!", a playful challenge to the girls' team. The girls seem impressed and clap for the boys, but as soon as the boys finish, the girls prepare to begin their own dance. When the music starts, the girls execute the moves with much greater accuracy and precision than the boys. All the boys watch the girls intently while bouncing to the beat.... [T]here is a general sense of enthusiasm and energy. Mr. Wagner [instructor] comments on it to me: "You see the intensity of their enthusiasm? The girls want to dance and the boys want to play, but for both, they are excited and very engrossed. The trick is to focus that enthusiasm. If we can do that, everybody wins."*

As the instructor of this apprenticeship has observed, the trick is to focus this enthusiasm, and organized group competitions seem to provide a good vehicle for accomplishing this objective. Moreover, setting up such competitions does not require exceptional instructor skills.

For apprenticeships in which acquired hard skills are not widely generalizable to other fields, particularly in the arts, the organized team competition approach could provide important benefits in the area of marketable job skills. Youth's experiences with group competition may provide opportunities to practice skills recognizable to potential employers as relevant to their needs (e.g., leadership, teamwork, problem solving), as well as vivid examples that youth could use when prompted for evidence of such skills in job interviews.

There are several implementation difficulties that may be anticipated with the competitive model. In a few of the apprenticeships, introducing group competition would involve a significant restructuring of the experience. In one or two instances, judges qualified to rate products or performances might not be readily available.

The most serious objection that may be encountered is that competition is incompatible with a positive youth development framework. Some of those who work in youth development, both leadership and staff, are not oriented toward even considering a strong competitive element in their programs. Competition is seen to have only a few winners but a large number of losers.[20] Many program youth have not been academic successes in school, and the program setting is seen by some instructors as presenting an alternative in which youth can thrive, resetting their development in a positive trajectory. So when we initially presented the findings about the benefits of organized group competition to ASM2009 supervisors and executives, some in the audience were stunned, with bewilderment evident in their questions to us and in their nonverbal reactions.

But it does not take long for any youth worker to recognize that many youth take naturally and eagerly to competition in sports, athletics more generally (e.g., foot races), and even in verbal games, such as playing the dozens, a popular activity among African American youth.[21] Competition is part of youth culture. Moreover, there are instances in many apprenticeships, which we presented in this chapter, where some form of competition does takes place and where the young people participate with enthusiasm.[22] Motivation and engagement go up, and youth workers can think of examples in their own practice where they have observed this. What we were able to tell them as outside evaluators is that the level of engagement in Elite

---

[20] The most frequently cited case against competition is Kohn (1992), who summarizes an extensive research base. There has been particular interest in whether competition diminishes intrinsic motivation (e.g., Reeve & Deci, 1996; Tauer & Harackiewicz, 1999), although much of this research is based on laboratory studies of college undergraduates.

[21] Playing the dozens features the verbal exchange of insults.

[22] We also found competition to take place often in Boys & Girls Clubs, a very different type of youth program than ASM2009 (see the twenty-five references to competition in the index to Hirsch, Deutch, & DuBois, 2011).

Eats during the competitive group cook-offs was higher – *by far* – than we observed on any occasion in any other apprenticeship. We cannot think of any instructor who would not want to see more youth engagement, and so this kind of information can be quite meaningful.

In countering objections to the value of competition, it is important to start with the fact that the competition is between groups rather than individuals. Teams were judged, not individuals. The fact that your team has lost does not mean that any one person as an individual did a bad job and should be seen as lower on the totem pole. Moreover, the judgment about which group was better was done by outsiders, who presumably do not have any favorites. The apprenticeship instructors made no ratings; they organized the competition, but were not the judges. This should minimize the potential for the outcome to negatively impact the relationship between any individual youth and the instructors. The structure isolates the instructors from judgment, allowing them a neutrality that makes it possible both to applaud the winning team and commiserate with the losing team.

Indeed, the nature of these organized group competitions corresponds well to findings from research on beneficial youth competition. In their reviews of the literature, the brothers David Johnson and Roger Johnson identified key characteristics of constructive competition, that is, elements of a competitive goal structure most likely to increase participants' effort to achieve, promote caring and committed relationships, and increase psychological health and well-being. These include (1) establishment of clear and specific rules, procedures, and criteria for winning; (2) a reasonable chance of winning for all participants; (3) opportunities for ongoing social comparison and monitoring of competitors' progress; and (4) an awareness of the unimportance of winning relative to the experience of fun and enjoyment.[23] These conditions correspond to the way that the group competition was organized in Elite Eats.

It is also important to recognize that the competition framework utilized in Elite Eats combined intragroup cooperation with intergroup competition. Provided the intergroup competition aspect does not overshadow the intragroup cooperation, research has found that intergroup competition can provide support and assistance, increase the enjoyment of competition, diffuse the responsibility for losing, and mitigate the negative impact of failure.[24] Relative to interpersonal competition and pure collaboration, *intergroup* competition can be the best of both worlds: it inspires high levels

[23] Johnson & Johnson (1989, 1999, 2005); Stanne, Johnson, & Johnson (1999).
[24] Johnson & Johnson (1999), p. 145.

of competence valuation, perceived challenge, and excitement characteristic of interpersonal competitive contexts, while also promoting the enthusiasm for meaningful interpersonal interaction characteristic of cooperation.[25]

Training instructors to implement organized team competition successfully seems reasonably straightforward and much easier than would be the case for authoritative mentoring. Instructors would benefit from an overview of the concept of appropriate competition and its positive outcomes, information that hopefully would assuage any doubts about introducing competitive activities within a youth-oriented program. Instructors would also benefit from explicit guidance on how to adapt their apprenticeship activities to the specific components of the organized team competition model and vice versa. For example, they could be given a sample rubric and the opportunity to create and receive feedback on rubrics specific to their own program activities. The tangible nature of core components for organized competition and the model's relative imperviousness to instructors' skills and attributes suggest that pre-service training could reasonably be accomplished in one or two workshops, in contrast to the multiple sessions required to do justice to the more nuanced and demanding authoritative mentorship model. The process of providing ongoing coaching and support for instructors would also be greatly simplified, as supervisory staff need only focus on an occasional, discrete activity as opposed to ongoing behavioral and relational norms.

Conceivably, if desired, the implementation of organized competition across program sites could be delegated to a specified staff person who functioned as a specialist, minimizing the need for instructor training and supervision. In this case, the designated staff person could be in charge of establishing competition parameters (in consultation with program instructors); organizing necessary supplies, judges, and an appropriate reward for winning teams; and monitoring activities on the day of the competition. This "outsourcing" of the model's implementation would not be possible for authoritative mentorship. Furthermore, delegating implementation of the model to a designated staff person might facilitate competition across similarly focused apprenticeships (e.g., dance), which could maximize collaboration within each program setting while still capitalizing on the benefits of a competitive framework. Such a possibility might appease instructors concerned that the competition model would disrupt the inclusive and family-like atmosphere they prioritize within their programs.

---

[25] Attle & Baker (2007); Tauer & Harackiewicz (2004); Wynne (1995).

Furthermore, the model might be rolled out over time. We suspect that instructors will be impressed with the level of youth engagement and learning that organized team competition elicits. The instructors chosen for the initial implementation could then serve as effective advocates to peers for scaling the model up. It would not require strong communication skills to explain the model and its benefits, as contrasted to the difficulties that might be expected in attempts to explain the much more complicated rationale for the authoritative mentoring approach.

The organized team competition model does not appear to create the same hiring dilemmas as anticipated for authoritative mentorship, as the requirements for specialized skills and attributes are much less. This mitigates the challenge of finding staff with expertise in both positive youth development and an occupational field, and also minimizes the negative impact of high staff turnover (at least as it applies to staff recruitment and the sustainability of the model).

SUMMARY

Both SongScape and Elite Eats stayed true to the ASM2009 framework in emphasizing skill development within a project-based framework. Both creatively used the overall rubric to create high-quality experiences that were linked to strong hiring outcomes on the mock job interview administered by HR professionals.

Both programs appear at first glance to be prime candidates to be adapted more broadly, within not only ASM2009 itself, but also the wider universe of organizations that seek to promote workforce development within a youth development framework. Nonetheless, our anticipatory implementation analysis – a critical analytic step before launching an ambitious new program – revealed stark differences in the likelihood of successful implementation. Put simply, we had trouble envisioning the successful implementation of the authoritative mentoring model; indeed, our analysis of the anticipated difficulties was, frankly, sobering. On the other hand, the organized team competition model appeared that it could be implemented well and without great cost. Competition is a well-known component of youth culture and this model appears to make good use of its positive dimensions while avoiding several potential problems.

5

What Human Resource Interviewers
Told Us about Youth Employability

I always had a great interest in what the twenty-eight human resource professionals who conducted the mock interviews thought of these youth's employability. To obtain this information, I conducted debriefing sessions after the day's interviews had been completed. Reports from these sessions are quoted extensively in this chapter to illustrate two types of behavior: first, how the young people often failed to communicate their strengths in the interview, and then how some youth did instead convincingly describe job-relevant skills. The quotes are presented accompanied initially by only modest commentary on my part. In the final sections of the chapter, I then consider the implications of the human resource (HR) findings for our understanding of why participation in After School Matters (ASM2009) did not result in superior performance on the mock job interview. I conclude by arguing that the HR findings should expand our views of the contributions that young people from these communities can make to the workforce.

In the debriefing sessions, the HR interviewers referred to youth responses during the formal part of the mock job interview as well as during a less formal feedback session that the interviewers provided to youth as thanks for their participation in this phase of the research. Although the interviewers could not use any information obtained during the feedback sessions in making their ratings, they were often struck by the information that emerged at that time. The discrepancy between what they were told during the formal interview and what they were told during the feedback portion of their session made a definite impression on them, which they told us about in the debriefing sessions.

I THOUGHT THIS DIDN'T "COUNT" AS WORK EXPERIENCE

The most consistent feedback that we received from the HR interviewers was that many of these young people did not know how to make a connection between the experiences they have had and the kinds of skills that were required for the job they had selected for the mock interview. The young people believed that if their experience did not come from a paid job, then it didn't "count." School activities, volunteer activities – none of that was thought to matter – so those experiences were frequently not mentioned in the interview.

The HR perspective was very different. The HR professionals wanted to know if you had certain skills. Even if those skills came outside of a paid employment situation, they counted. But these young people did not know that.

> HR interviewer: *I think they just don't know. When you tell them they're like, oh, yeah, but no one's ever told them that.*

Even family experiences could count:

> HR: *I don't want to limit it to jobs, because I do think that if you are responsible for feeding all your siblings every night and you are fifteen [years old] then that is phenomenal experience ... it doesn't have to be paid.*

Economists Philip Moss and Chris Tilly had similar findings in a study of employers. They quote a representative from an insurance company that was hiring for entry-level jobs, talking about HS graduates:

> "If it is a new hire, a trainee kind of thing, they are likely not to have had much work experience for that level of position. So we are going to be looking for them to demonstrate to us how they may have in the past been able to use those skills, whether it was leading a Girl Scout troop or what it may be."[1]

There were many aspects to this lack of understanding that frustrated our interviewers. One focused on basic academic experiences that youth had in school. A substantial body of research has focused on how scores on standardized tests predict later-life achievement in employment.[2] But that was

---

[1] Moss & Tilly (2001), p. 231.
[2] Lazear (2003); Mulligan (1999); Murnane et al. (2000).

not what concerned the HR folk. It was that these students would often have no idea how academics of any sort could bear on their employability:

> HR: *Nobody said, "I could do this job because I've had computer classes or I'm good at math." They don't relate any course work to jobs. They knew that grades were important, but they don't know why.*

Indeed, several interviewers told us of students who proudly told them of their grade point average (GPA). They knew that like the back of their hand. But that did not mean that these same students could relate the skills they had learned in class to employment situations.

The ability to organize and prioritize is a soft skill that the interviewers cited in this regard. The HR assumption was that to get good grades, and to complete complex, longer-term assignments that the students had in school, such softs skills had to have been utilized. But they were not brought up. Organizing skills could also be learned in many other settings, but again were unlikely to be brought up by students if they did not think experiences in those settings counted:

> HR: *You really did have to pull it out of them. Because I did, when I was asking them about experience, I would transition to, "let's talk about community work that you do, some volunteerism you do in the community or church with family," you know, and as I opened that can of worms up, it started to come out. Well I've done this. Well, what did you do with that? Did you have to plan and organize something? And then they started to see it.*

Planning and organizing were far from the only skills that these young people had developed. One of the mock jobs involved sales at our fictional store, Chicago Cool Clothes. Some of the students who applied for a Cool Clothes job had participated in an ASM2009 apprenticeship in Web design. Now, at first glance, it does seem like a bit of a stretch to link computer programming with selling clothes at a retail outlet. But it is not if you consider the specific design of that apprenticeship. Apprentices had to create their own website based on one of their hobbies or special interests and the site had to involve selling merchandise related to that interest. There were sites for cars and athletic shoes and cosmetics and all kinds of products. The apprentices took great pride in how attractively they had designed their site. When I came to visit the apprenticeship, several of them rushed up to me and took me to their computer to show off their site. So an essential component of their apprenticeship was marketing and sales, and what they needed to do in the interview was make the connection between their acquired on-line sales skills with the sales skills needed for the retail site. But they did not think that way:

> HR: *They also had difficulty articulating how what they did would help them get a job, so they're not able to put that experience [to use] … If you went to After School Matters, that's great. Tell me what you did. But you really had to pull that out. They didn't understand that you need to put that on the table and then make the connection to [how] the skill that you learned in After School Matters is going to help you in this job, even though what you're applying for is Cool Clothes and in After School Matters you learned web design. How is that going to help you? And that was the missing piece. They could not make that connection.*

Sales related experiences could be gained in many settings besides ASM2009. This interviewer returned to how frequently these skills seemed to be obtained in high school classes, a setting not limited to ASM2009 participants, in which important job skills were being acquired:

> HR: *And so, for the Cool Clothes, part of it was setting out the displays, and I said, "Have you ever had to do a poster board for a presentation for class?" Yeah. I said, "So that's designing and marketing. Your poster board would be the same or similar skill to setting up a display of merchandise." And they were like, "Ohhhhh." So they don't think about the thing that they've done. When they hear the word "experience," I think they think work experience or job experience. And so I was getting a lot of "I don't have any experience."*

In addition to recognizing the job value of particular experiences, the youth's communication skills were important as well. In many instances, the young people would assert that they had particular skills without providing any evidence. This did not impress the HR professionals:

> *You tell me you're hard working, but when were you hard working ….*
> *I want them to prove it! I want the proof. How will you prove you're a conscientious student? What are your grades? What are you taking? How do you get through it?*

TEAMWORK AND LEADERSHIP

One of the most important aspects of the contemporary workplace that the HR professionals highlighted for us involved teamwork. Coordinating activities, respecting the diversity that characterizes workplaces in urban settings, helping each other out, problem solving when issues arose – all of these are essential to organizational functioning and productivity. Similar conclusions have been reached in a host of other reports.[3] Part of teamwork at times involves exercising leadership, taking the initiative in pushing things forward, and breaking through barriers that are inhibiting team performance. The fact that even young people could provide such leadership is consistent with a model of leadership that sees such behavior as distributed across a team and not merely the preserve of the person nominally in charge.[4]

In terms of teamwork and leadership, our HR interviewers were sometimes left pulling their hair out as youth often did not make obvious tie-ins to their prior experiences; at the same time, there were some youth who were able to discuss positive examples that impressed the interviewers. Let us consider first some examples of young people's failure to recognize relevant prior experiences. In this area, perhaps nothing frustrated the interviewers more than when the youth had been on an athletic team but did not bring it up.

> HR1: *She seemed to love basketball, she couldn't link that to, why does she want to work at Cool Clothes, what experience, I mean just nothing ... so eventually ... I'm like ok, tell me some of the things you do as a captain because at one point she was a captain ... I said that's leadership, it's responsibility, do you have to be disciplined? ... so I think once I kind of put it out there, she was like "Oh, ok" ... But she just couldn't connect until I put it out there, you know the discipline, the teamwork, and all that, then she kind of got it. Yeah, I had several boys that were on football and one that was on football and basketball and I didn't know until the very end when I was giving them feedback or by probing on a question. So again, I don't think they know how to relate all those skills they learn on a sports team [to] the workplace.*
>
> HR2: *[In] the case of volunteers, they are just not seeing where being a leader can [mean] be[ing] a leader on a basketball [team], they are just totally missing that, and how that leadership skill can be used for a summer job. They just totally don't see it. And it's for a lot of students, they just totally don't see that.*
>
> HR3: *Those are [instances] again where they couldn't connect the sports experiences [to a job]. That's a lot of teamwork. That's really impressive to an employer at least in my experience when you're looking at [someone] that has no work experience but they've been on basketball and volleyball.*

---

[3] Casner-Lotto & Barrington (2006); Murnane & Levy (1996); SCANS (1991).
[4] Spillane (2006). See Larson (2000) for the importance of initiative in adolescent development.

At the same time, there were positive examples of teamwork and leadership that some youth did highlight. The first example I will quote came from a young woman who demonstrated excellent skills in project management. Now "project management" is not something that you think of with respect to a high school student working with others on a school project. But the HR professional saw project management skills – skills that are important and highly valued in the workplace, and by no means just in entry level jobs – in the example:

> HR: ... *she was a potential project manager. You can just tell that she's somebody who knows how to break down tasks. So it was on a specific science project on, or no, in a literature project that they worked on. And she was able to recognize [the member] of the team who had special skill sets, who knew how to do PowerPoint, who knew how to write well, who knew how to present well, and she broke down the tasks for everybody. And then when they all had to regroup, she facilitated. You know, asked them questions on how did you prepare this. So that she would draw from the team what they learned from each of the tasks they had performed, so collectively they all knew what they were doing. I just thought it was a pretty decent response. It was [being] a good project manager and leader-facilitator.*

Another important part of being an effective part of a team is to help disaffected team members reconnect. Here is an example of a male student who knew there was an angry team member, spent extra time with him, and helped him to rejoin the team and contribute to it:

> HR: *[he] said they were working on a group project and there was one student that was very disengaged and very angry and wouldn't do anything for the project, so this young man decided he was gonna walk home with him from school one day and find out what was going on. So he walked home with him, found out he was having some trouble at home and just kind of made himself available to him. And then after that conversation he came back to school and was engaged in the project and they ended up getting a great grade .... I just thought it very mature for his age to do something like that.*

Yes, it was a mature thing to do. Yet it is hardly beyond a teenager's capacity. Teens are noted for close friendships and that is one of the things that friends do for each other.[5] In this instance, the young man transferred those interpersonal skills very effectively to a school work group. And the HR

---

[5] See Brown & Larson (2009) for a review of the literature on adolescent friendships.

interviewer had no trouble envisaging how those same skills could be valuable on the job. This person was not the only student to display these types of mature leadership skills. For example,

> HR: *she accepted the responsibility as the leader in the group. The way she articulated it was very much like speaking to an adult. It wasn't at a high school level …*

The way in which both of these HR professionals were impressed by the maturity of these youth is worth noting. Maturity was one of the variables that we had interviewers rate at the conclusion of each interview. In statistical analyses, we examined the correlation of all of the individual variables in the interview with the interviewer's judgment as to whether they would hire the youth for a full-time job. It turned out that maturity had a very strong correlation with hiring ($r = .82$) and, indeed, was the strongest predictor of hiring in our data set (see Chapter 2 for a more complete report).

The final example in this section has to do with team leadership skills displayed by a young person who was on the quiet side. Quiet teens are not the type one thinks of in terms of leadership. But this individual made very effective use of his personality:

> HR: *He tends to be quiet and so he said that in the group he was the one encouraging quiet people to contribute. He thought that it was important that everyone contribute and he identified that some people are shy in groups and he needs to ask them questions. And at the end of the group project everyone had contributed and had shared their opinion, and he was the team leader.*

Getting all team members to contribute is an important task and this young person drew on his unique perspective to make sure that happened. One could imagine that this is the type of person who might bring distinctive contributions to work sites as well.

THE YOUNG PERSON'S ANALYTIC SKILLS AND DECISION MAKING

One of the most interesting and important debriefing sessions came at the conclusion of our third and final year of data collection. It is not surprising that this discussion would come during the final debriefing session. It took me a while to understand how HR professionals think and to place the youth interview responses within that context. The material in this debriefing session went beyond what had been discussed before and

I pushed the interviewers to elaborate on their answers more than I had. What follows is a fairly lengthy transcript of the most interesting part of that session. I copy this section in its entirety because it addresses critical issues concerning the potential impact these young people – all of whom are low-income, urban youth, and almost all minority – can have in the world of work. The session begins when I note that I have repeatedly heard that interviewers want to hear "elaborated answers" from youth. [Note that many different HR professionals were part of this conversation, but each is referred to as "HR."]

> *Bart Hirsch: One of the things I've heard a lot is that sometimes, for some of these questions, the answer isn't in some ways as important, it's not like there's a correct answer. But what's important is how the person thought about it, and that they really thought things through, and were able to analyze things and what you want is really the elaborated answer that shows somebody's thinking. What I don't ... and people are shaking their heads 'yes' for the most part ...*
>
> *Group: Yes, absolutely.*
>
> *Bart Hirsch: ... Now this is what I don't have and which I need in your words. Why is that important? What does it show, what does that kind of an answer demonstrate that is of value in the business world?*
>
> *HR: The "get it" factor, I think for me. I mean, it's like there is a "get it" factor. They're thinking through the question and the process, even if maybe the answer is not absolutely thorough or fantastic.*
>
> *Bart Hirsch: How is that going to be useful in the business world?*
>
> *HR: Well in the business world there will be many outcomes that won't be exactly what you like and so the goal is to be able to have that thought process to think it through, to evaluate your options, to learn from what you did in the past and move forward to improve upon what happens. So that ability, that analytic ability, the decision making ability, the ability to learn from your past, to take some risks, right? You want people in business to take risks, if they take no risks nothing will change. So that's what you're really looking for ... not the right answer, the right answer gets you more of the same.*
>
> *Bart Hirsch: Right, sometimes there's not a right answer. You don't know what the answer is at all ...*
>
> *HR: Sometimes there's not a right answer.*
>
> *Bart Hirsch: ... something that's likely to generate a good answer and move things forward.*
>
> *HR: It gives you insight into the way they think, [the] way they make decisions. To me it's a sign of maturity. I'm impressed when I see a freshman in high school who thinks things through before they take action.*

Bart Hirsch: OK, and tell me again, and again I'm asking it, sometimes I know the answer but I need it in your own words. Why is that good, in the business world? Why is it that someone who does that, why is that someone likely to be successful in the business world?

HR: If you don't have maturity, don't use that process in thinking, you're likely to make mistakes, you're not likely to recognize when you make a mistake, I think others will be disturbed by your … it's not impatience, but kinda jumping into things, leaping in without any thinking about the consequences (someone interjects: impulsiveness). Yes, impulsiveness can really be a negative impact in the workplace.

HR: Absolutely, I think leaders and qualities of leaders, it's critical thinking skills. Natural leaders have the ability to kind of think big picture and break things down. Like this [young] woman, I mean, it's an example there of a leader, of somebody that is looking at the bigger picture and then breaking it down to execute ….

Bart Hirsch: I just want to push you a little more, again just to make it explicit …. How is that important, all these things in the business world. What will someone accomplish who has those abilities versus someone who doesn't have those abilities.

HR: Well, you can probably speak to this in your own area, I would just say, leadership … I would say somebody can accomplish taking on either managing people … managing of a function, leadership responsibility, learning new things … I think they just demonstrate [that] they're just not afraid to learn new areas and [this is important because] change in the workplace is continuously happening. So somebody who has that ability to be not risk averse, who's willing to go out there and try new things is a tremendous asset to businesses today, because they're not afraid to do it. So a leader, somebody with those skills and attributes, are gonna be natural high potentials in an organization, because they have those critical thinking skills, they have the ability to learn new areas within an organization, they're not afraid of change, they're not risk averse and they're natural teachers. So I think they just have an ability to learn things, absorb knowledge, and then teach others. Those are tremendous qualities that organizations probably are lacking a lot of in leadership today that I think would be tremendous assets to companies.

HR: If I could just add to that, I had a student who couldn't make a decision in terms of what to say, she had all these experiences to build on and just couldn't pull out the one she needed to communicate. So I guess in terms of the business world it's good that you're thinking through the process, but if you never make a decision and never act on it, it's not beneficial.

HR: I see it in a very different light, because from the HR perspective, I always worry about somebody who doesn't know how to manage themselves. And what I mean about that is when you hire someone and that person

expects their manager to identify their skills, identify their strengths, provide training, be the person who is responsible for their career success and
I think that's too passive. It's not going to get them anywhere. So as an HR
professional whenever I go anywhere, I tell my employees, it's your job to
manage up. And if you can't articulate what you're good at and what you
can do, your manager is never going to pick you if he or she is not a good
listener and doesn't pay enough attention to you, which is very common.
So if you can put yourself out there in the spotlight and provide all the
details that your manager needs, you make your manager's job that much
easier and you get the promotion. That's my interest, are people getting
promoted for the right skill set and not just because they are the manager's
favorite.

Bart: So kids, people who have these qualities in the workplace are going to
be more successful and they're going to be promoted more often [and] more
likely to be promoted into leadership positions.

HR: Yeah, I think if you answer the question right, and right means providing
all the details, and the story and the context, then people get to know you
better, and they put you in the right place ... Versus they assume you can't
do the job because you weren't able to articulate your strengths and then
you don't get that opportunity.

HR: What I also saw was a correlation between their thinking process and
the quality of their answers. So in fact, this last one I had, just flip answers,
didn't do any thinking, and the answers often were not to the questions.
After a while I had to give up. But the kids who thought things through
could answer all the questions with good thinking, good answers, and detail.
So in the workplace, to get back to the workplace, I would assume that if
I hired those people they would think things through before they took action,
they would have recommendations to make things better ... and they would
be confident because they would find success after success.

HR: I know I've said this to you before but the kids are very interested in giving the right answer and they focus more on the right answer instead of all
the other things they've learned in the process and the process is the product.
And the more they could learn [that] the process is the product, it's not the
volcano [referring to a school science project], it's not the written report, it's
not the PowerPoint presentation ... it's the process of how it happened that
will make them be more desirable for employers and quite frankly make
them be employable and able to earn a living.

To unpack what the HR interviewers meant when they said that they
wanted the youth to give "elaborated" answers, I asked the HR professionals to elaborate on what *they* meant by elaborated answers and their
importance. From multiple individuals, we heard a clear consensus. At its
core, elaborated answers to job interview questions revealed the candidate's

analytic and critical thinking skills. The priority given to such youth skills has been testified to frequently in prior studies of top corporate executives and the HR professionals were on the same page.[6] The young person's skills could be demonstrated in response to a behavioral question, which probed what he or she had done in an actual prior situation. These skills could also be demonstrated in response to a question asking what they would do in a hypothetical future situation. By discussing their responses in detail, the young people revealed their thought processes, how they approached the situation, how they understood it, what options they considered, the action(s) they took, and what happened as a result of their actions.

It should be emphasized that more than analytical ability is being referenced. A prime concern was also the youth's decision-making process. How was their understanding of the situation linked to their actions? Why did they take the actions they did (or would take, for hypothetical situations)? How did they address the interpersonal and other aspects of the situation? Did they discuss their actions calmly and confidently, or were they uncertain and likely to elicit doubt among those they needed to work with? Finally, what did they learn from the outcome – even if it was not as positive as they might have liked – so that they could do better the next time? Some of the examples that were cited earlier in the chapter regarding teamwork and leadership exemplify some of these experiences and skills.

Action is critical and change in business practices is necessary. The employee who is willing to take the risks to make things better for the organization – and not everyone is willing or able to do this, and to do it effectively – is critical to business success. Successful risk takers are "high potentials" for the firm and just the type of person you would want to hire and promote from entry-level positions.

IMPLICATIONS FOR THE AFTER SCHOOL
MATTERS EVALUATION

The data from debriefing the HR professionals suggest another factor, beyond those identified in Chapter 3, that could have led to the lack of significant findings. Many of the youth, whether they had been in ASM2009 or not, had experiences and skills that employers would value, but the youth themselves often did not know this and did not communicate those strengths in the mock job interview.

---

[6] Casner-Lotto & Barrington (2006).

If this HR analysis is accurate, then we can see that ASM2009 made faulty assumptions in believing that participation in their apprenticeships would automatically lead to marketable job skills. The core of the problem, as reflected in the HR debriefings, is in the assumption that learning job skills, by itself, is sufficient to make those skills marketable.

This assumption fell apart for two reasons. The youth often were not aware that what they learn in the apprenticeships is of value to employers. They did not recognize that the skills that they had been taught were in fact job skills. Teenagers need to be told – frankly, they need to be convinced – that employers will value what they are learning. And they need to understand the reasons why employers will appreciate those experiences and skills, the value that they bring to the workplace. But no one told them this. We observed countless apprenticeship sessions and the instructors did not typically refer to actual workplaces. They did not tell the young people that these were job skills that employers sought. Other studies also have found that teenagers are confused about the nature of adult jobs.[7]

The Web design apprenticeship is a good example of this communication failure. In learning how to create websites for selling merchandise, the apprentices had developed a skill that could earn them money immediately. They could market those skills to local businesses right away. And certainly there are careers that are available in that line of work that they could enter. Yet the instructors not only did not emphasize this, but they also barely mentioned it at all. In our experience, the only time when it was brought up was when a guest lecturer talked about it during his visit.

Another faulty assumption was that teenagers would know how to communicate relevant experiences and skills in a job interview situation. But many of the teens did not know how to give the elaborated answers that the HR interviewers valued. So even if they had recognized the job skills that they had learned, many youth were not able to communicate them successfully. As we shall see in the next chapter, these are skills that can be taught, but they were not taught in ASM2009.

Many ASM2009 youth appear to have gotten job skills from their apprenticeships and that is a major accomplishment. But the conclusion from the HR data is clear: ASM2009 did not provide job skills that were sufficiently *marketable*.

---

[7] Csikszentmihalyi & Schneider (2000). See Schoon & Silbereisen (2009) on the confusing nature of the school-to-work transition more generally.

OBJECTIONS

The HR interviewers believed that these young people had skills that would be valuable in the workplace and that some youth were quite talented indeed. Before we consider the broader significance of these findings, we ought first to take a "time out" and consider a variety of objections that, essentially, argue against putting much faith in these data. This will permit us to surface concerns about the underlying basis for our findings in the mock job interview that go beyond issues considered in Chapter 2. These are legitimate scientific issues even if such concerns can sometimes be used for ideological purposes. To address these objections we will need to switch gears a bit and move away from the study of interview transcripts and take a more argumentative perspective.

Problems with the Interview Itself

First is the possibility that our sample of HR interviewers was biased, that they were simply a bunch of leftist do-gooders who would hire anyone with a minority or poverty background. Our project did attract HR professionals who volunteered their time without pay, and they may have been more interested in issues concerning low-income, minority youth than the average HR worker. Even if this is true, all the evidence I have is that they were hard-nosed business folk. They focused on whether a young person would or would not serve the *employer's* interest. In debriefing sessions, they frequently brought up why a specific youth was unsuitable for employment.

Another objection is that the HR interviewers essentially based their judgment on stories that youth told, stories that might have been fabricated. It is true that youth's stories played an important role in influencing hiring ratings. It is also true that stories told by witnesses in a court of law form the basis of civil and criminal verdicts reached by juries in our system of justice. We rely on juries to judge the credibility of witnesses, using their common sense intelligence. The HR interviewers were highly concerned with the credibility of what they were told by youth, just as they are in actual employment interviews with adults. They asked for lots of concrete detail, probed the responses they got, and paid careful attention to nonverbal cues to assess truthfulness. The interviewers were on the lookout for "canned" answers that youth might have been taught to tell in interviews. The HR interviewers asserted that they had a professional obligation not to be fooled, which they took very seriously. Here is what one interviewer said worried her the most in the interviews:

> *If I felt like they were just bullshitting me. If they're bullshitting me in the interview, I don't know what they're going to do in my business. They might steal from me, they might, you know, they might do something unsafe.*

This representative view strikes me as coming from someone who was very careful about what she heard and did not mind using plain language to make sure that the importance of this point was appreciated.

Another objection centers on the fact that we relied on HR personnel, though many interviews for entry-level jobs are done by supervisors. It is true that supervisors play a very important role in the hiring process, but HR professionals are often very much involved as well. Moreover, we know from other studies that supervisors, too, often rely on brief job interviews and prefer that method over information gained by other means.[8]

Aren't School Grades More Important?

One might wonder whether we should be looking at mock job interviews in the first place. Are not scores on standardized tests or school grades more credible than what youth say in an interview? Standardized test scores and grades are related to various employment measures on average, but the association is not a strong one.[9] We examined this in our own data among both ASM2009 and control group youth. We found a statistically significant, but weak correlation between youth's prior standardized test scores and whether they would be hired for a permanent job on the mock job interview ($r = .10$, $p < .05$, $N = 419$).[10]

Given that modest correlation, we expected to find that many of the students who were hired in the mock interview did not have great grades. Let's look at the grades from the last high school in our sample, the one whose students were the subject of so much of the HR enthusiasm in our last debriefing session. Indeed, let's look at the students who received the highest rating possible (a 5) on the hiring scale, whom the interviewers would have hired *with enthusiasm* (hire with enthusiasm was required for making a 5 rating). The students with a hiring rating of 5 turn out to be

---

[8] Rosenbaum (2001). See also Holzer (1966) on the importance of job interviews for hiring low-income youth in business.

[9] Currie & Thomas (1999); Rose (2006); Roth, BeVier, Switzer III, & Schippmann (1996).

[10] Drawing on archival data from Chicago Public Schools, our measure of a young person's standardized test score was an average of the two most recent assessments (averaged over reading and math).

C students (median weighted GPA = 2.16). Moreover, according to their transcripts, 38 percent of those who received a score of 5 on the hiring variable on the mock job interview had less than a 2.0 GPA. Those are not good grades.[11]

Academic measures provide uncertain information (or "signals") regarding the ability of a specific applicant to do well on a specific job, so it is not surprising that the association lacks strength. Students may be very good at "book learning," but this does not tell us much about how well they will do in the real world faced with ambiguous situations and emotional people. The artificial situations used as test items in standardized tests are a long way from what is needed on most jobs, and the transferability of much school knowledge to other situations is typically not high.[12] By contrast, the mock job interview assesses real-world challenges and actions, and allows interviewers to probe responses, allowing for a deeper and more fine-grained analysis.

Research that Focuses on Youth Deficiencies

Finally, let's consider findings from a frequently cited study by Jill Casner-Lotto and Linda Barrington that takes a more negative view of youth abilities.[13] This study collected data from high-level HR executives in 431 US firms on the workforce skills of America's youth. The report chose to emphasize the deficiencies of young people, especially those who have only a high school degree, as if a deficit orientation was the only one that made sense. However, there are serious problems with their methodology that undermine the report. The response rate for the survey was a mere 4.8 percent, which indicates that the data come from an extremely small percentage of all those who received the questionnaire. Frankly, it is one of the lowest response rates I have ever seen for a survey in any field of research.[14] It is illegitimate and irresponsible to draw conclusions – presumptuously

---

[11] Sometimes the interviewers knew the students' grades, typically when a student with a high GPA would volunteer it in the interview. Otherwise, interviewers themselves did not typically inquire about the GPA. In not doing so, they were representative of most businesses, where other researchers, using other methods, have found that people making hiring decisions had little interest in high school grades or obtaining transcripts (Rosenbaum, 2001).

[12] Perkins & Salomon (1992); Salomon & Perkins (1989).

[13] Casner-Lotto & Barrington (2006).

[14] The paper would likely not have gotten through the peer review process that is required for publication in scholarly journals.

labeled a Report Card – about the workforce preparation of a nation's youth from such a study.

Even though there are serious problems with their sample, do not the data that Casner-Lotto and Barrington obtain provide useful information about the work skills of young people?[15] I would pay far more attention to the findings if the respondents had based their replies on a systematic review of their hires, drawing heavily on reports from front-line supervisors. But there is nothing in the report to indicate that this occurred. The surveys were likely to have been considered "paperwork" that should be gotten through quickly (or not at all, for most of those who received an invitation to participate). Survey respondents are notorious for zipping through questions at Olympic speed. Under such circumstances, respondents are likely to draw on stereotypes, which would point to presumed deficits.

Of course, many low-income, urban youth are not adequately prepared for the labor market. These young people often continue to experience difficulty in getting a job as adults.[16] We know that in Chicago, youth who apply to ASM2009 – which, in this study, includes both the intervention and control groups – have better academic records than those who do not, and that many Chicago youth in public high schools do not even apply for the program.[17] Youth who are not in any structured after-school program may well be less motivated for employment and have fewer work readiness skills.

However, this study has identified two other groups whose existence argues against a simple deficit view. One of those groups involves young people who have gained experiences and skills that would be valued in the workplace, but do not know that and do not communicate those skills adequately in (mock) job interviews. The second group are young people who have accumulated important experiences and skills, *and* are able to communicate those well. Some of those youth are highly prized by HR professionals. These two important groups are swept under the rug in deficit-oriented reports that distort our understanding of the developmental transition into adulthood and, ultimately, severely curtail policy options.

Let us close this section by noting that even if the findings from our research are credible, they do not represent the final word. We have to

---

[15] It is important to note that I am critiquing here that aspect of the report that focuses on employer judgments about youth work skills. I think that the study's report on employers' views about the needs of employers is more credible and reference the study elsewhere in that regard.

[16] Moss & Tilly (2001).

[17] Goerge et al. (2007). Indeed, many Chicago high school youth are not involved in any structured after-school activity (George, Chaskin, & Guiltinan, 2005).

replicate the results with different interviewers, different youth, in different locations, and with different (mock) jobs. But until we get those data, these findings need to be highlighted in a wider-ranging discussion of how we understand the contributions that low-income, minority youth can make to the workplace.

RACIAL DISCRIMINATION?

There is nothing in the data presented earlier in the chapter to suggest that there was racial discrimination. This is a factor that needs to be considered whenever addressing minority employability.[18] We have not yet spoken to this issue in part because we have had so few nonminority youth in the two programs we studied. There were literally only a handful of nonminority youth in the ASM2009 research (99.1 percent of the sample were either African American or Hispanic), and no more than that in the job interviewing training program. Had there been appreciably more nonminority youth, we would have compared their hiring rates and so on to those of minority youth. But the nature of the sample precluded such analyses.

When I talked to HR interviewers between and after the interviews, I did query them from time to time about the communication styles of the African American youth. From my prior research at Boys & Girls Clubs, I knew that youth in these communities often spoke what is termed vernacular African American English. From that research, I had become acquainted with some of the scholarly literature in that area and had devoted part of a chapter in my first book to an analysis of how one staff member had effectively used such speech in mentoring youth at the club.[19] It was natural for me to wonder, and for several of my colleagues to ask me, whether youth had used vernacular African American English in their interviews and whether this had any impact on the HR interviewers.

Some of the interviewers indicated that such speech patterns had come up in their interviews. When it did, the interviewers all seemed to have a similar response: it was no big deal. The HR professionals noted it, but did not deem it of any special salience. They did not ignore it, but it was just one factor among many in making a judgment about a young person's communication ability. Youth's use of this cultural pattern of expression, when it occurred, did not appear to lead to stereotypical portrayals and poorer ratings.

---

[18] See, for example, Moss & Tilly (1996, 2001).
[19] Hirsch (2005), see chapter 4.

DIVERSITY AND TALENT IN THE WORKPLACE

The natural tendency, when thinking of youth such as those in our research, coming from low-income minority families, and receiving their education in a large-city school system, would be to worry. Way behind on many standard measures of academic achievement, they can seem hopelessly ill prepared to land a job in our modern, highly competitive, global economy. But the HR professionals thought a good number of them would be hirable. How could that be?

As we just discussed, it was not because of their academics. Instead, the interviewers judged the mock hires to be hirable on the basis of their soft skills. They were enthusiastic about hiring the students with a 5 rating because of their analytical and critical thinking skills, their excellent teamwork and leadership skills, and their ability to be prudent risk-takers in uncertain situations. The HR interviewers made these judgments based on their professional appraisal of the youth's prior experiences. Good youth programs provide excellent contexts for learning these skills.[20]

Similar positive appraisals of the workforce readiness of minority urban youth were found in a study that Stephanie Riger and I conducted several years ago. We interviewed the work supervisors of three dozen high school youth who were working at summer jobs at major Chicago firms.[21] Although the top-level executives of those firms were skeptical that the summer hires were hirable for full-time positions, the supervisors told us emphatically that, based on their performance over the summer, they would hire these youth for full-time jobs. Even more strikingly, they told us that they would *prefer* to hire these young people for open positions rather than the in-company transfers who were typically hired.

Our own findings are consistent with those from a number of economists who have studied the importance of what they refer to as noncognitive skills in much larger, longitudinal samples. Noncognitive skills, similar to what we have been referring to as soft skills, are distinct from the capacity to solve abstract problems and from traditional measures of human capital, such as years of education and training.[22] These measures of social skills and of personality characteristics (motivation, persistence, emotional stability,

---

[20] Larson & Angus (2011) provide a detailed account of how this happens in good youth programs, focusing on the development of strategic thinking.

[21] Hirsch & Riger (1989).

[22] Linqvist & Vestman (2011). Psychologists would assert that many so-called noncognitive skills do in fact involve cognitive factors.

etc.) have been found to predict future labor market outcomes, including finding employment. Noncognitive skills seem to have an especially strong effect among those who receive low wages, which seems consistent with our research given our focus on entry-level positions.[23]

These data suggest that the pool of potential youth hires is greater than would be suggested by reliance on grades and test scores – or from the stereotypes of top executives in quick surveys. Businesses lose out when they fail to assess youth's soft skills. When you look at the full skill set, the pool of eligible youth is considerably greater than had been thought. Of course, not all youth have the requisite skills and we should not ignore that group.[24] But there is a paucity of eligible youth from these communities only if you put on blinders to the real skills these young people would bring to many of today's service sector jobs.

It should be clear that we are not talking solely of meeting criteria for entry level jobs. When the HR professionals talked admiringly of some youths' higher level analytical and decision-making skills, they were talking of young people who had management potential. These were youth that they could see having "success after success" and who would be a firm's "high potentials." From the HR debriefings, the number of youth who have this high potential is a subset of those who are deemed hirable, but it is important to appreciate that those youth are out there when you would think, from all that is said and written, that they do not even exist.

Furthermore, that soft skills (or noncognitive skills) are an important resource for managers is borne out in a number of predictive studies. Economists have found that wage differentials among managers are impacted by levels of noncognitive skills, especially social skills that are useful in managing or motivating groups of people.[25] Psychologists who have studied this issue in longitudinal studies have also found that young people with good social skills experience more work success later in life.[26]

---

[23] Almlund et al. (2011); Duckworth et al. (2014); Duckworth, Heckman & Rubinstein (2001); Heckman et al. (2006); Kuhn & Weinberger (2005); Lindqvist & Vestman (2011); Waddell (2006). See also Bowles, Gintis, & Osbourne (2001).

[24] DeCoursey & Skyles (2007) discuss the need for comprehensive services to prepare these youth for the workforce.

[25] Kuhn and Weinberger (2005) studied the subsequent labor market outcomes of youth who held leadership positions in high school. Lindqvist and Vestman (2011) followed the labor market histories of Swedish military recruits who were interviewed by a psychologist.

[26] Masten et al. (2010).

There is sometimes the thought that to hire low-income minority youth from urban communities is really doing a public service, charity as it were, that does not make business sense. The HR professionals told us something very different. They told us that it was in the firm's best business interest to hire many of these youth because the youth would bring problem-solving and leadership skills to the firm. The firm would derive long-term benefit from having more of these young people on board as decision makers.

As detailed earlier in this chapter, many young people did not recognize that they had business-relevant experiences and skills and thus did not bring them up in the interview. This is a crucial developmental skill that they had not acquired. If those young people could learn to recognize that employers value that skill set and if they could be trained to communicate their credentials effectively in an employment interview, then the pool of hirable workers would be enlarged even more. In the next chapter, we discuss a program we developed to accomplish these objectives and its initial implementation in Chicago Public Schools.

The broadest conclusion we draw from our debriefing of the HR interviewers is consistent with the emphasis on positive youth development that has emerged in recent years in much of the academic and practice communities. A deficit orientation does injustice to the many competent youth in our communities. It not only short-changes them and their families, but also unnecessarily constrains the labor pool that business can draw upon. Rather than disparaging young people, businesses ought to devote more effort to identifying and recruiting those young people who have talents that add value to the workplace.

6

A Program for Teaching Youth How to
Do Well in Job Interviews

This book is concerned with new program directions for helping low-income minority youth enter the workforce. We first discussed After School Matters (ASM), which shares with many other programs an emphasis on providing youth with job-related training and experiences. What is different about ASM is that it provides these as part of an after-school program for high school students. In evaluating ASM2009, we identified areas where programmatically more needed to be done. We noted especially that the human resource (HR) interviewers found that many youth did not understand that the skills that they had developed would be valued in the workplace and, furthermore, did not know how to communicate them effectively in the mock job interview. Many workforce development programs provide some interview training, and all of the ASM2009 apprentices in our evaluation were exposed to at least one such session. But it did not seem enough.

There appears to be a mismatch between youth's expectations and understanding of the interview and what the HR interviewers require. Many young people have not developed the crucial developmental skill of being able to translate their background into ways that make sense to HR professionals, the gatekeepers who often decide whether someone is ready to enter the workforce. Put another way, youth need to acquire transfer or bridging skills that allow them to show how their prior experiences will enable them to meet new challenges in a different environment.[1] What is needed are more effective programs that focus on how to help youth acquire these skills. The employment interview has a culture of its own, and young

---

[1] This calls to mind Wilson's (2012) finding that young people in these communities are often isolated from mainstream social networks in which extended family, for example, might serve as role models or sources of information about entry into different segments of the labor market.

people need to understand what "counts" as relevant experience, which experiences are worth bringing up and which should be kept to themselves, and the particular way in which interviewers prefer to hear them discuss their experiences. Having just conducted several hundred mock job interviews with high school students, and having ready access to the acquired wisdom and expertise of a host of HR professionals, we were in an excellent position to develop a program to teach these skills.

The opportunity to develop this program came with the appointment of a new CEO of Chicago Public Schools. He brought in his own top-level management group and I was well acquainted with one of the individuals on that team. Soon, I was talking with another new hire, who reported directly to the CEO, who had responsibility for a majority of high school students. This administrator was excited about what could be gained from the mock job interview. She offered me the opportunity to develop the program in a number of different areas that she directed and I chose to do so in Career and Technical Education. I chose that area because she had just appointed a new leader who was eager to try new approaches. All was going well until I was asked to begin piloting the program in three months. This was much sooner than I had anticipated! But not wanting to look a gift horse in the mouth, and knowing that I could quickly assemble a good HR team to support the effort, I agreed.

HR TASK FORCE

I assembled a task force of the most insightful HR interviewers from the ASM2009 evaluation, ensuring that there was some diversity among them in terms of the type of business or nonprofit in which they worked, and their own race and ethnicity. We went over each question in the mock interview in detail and probed for the range of possible positive responses. I would continually ask, "What if a young person said X?" or "What if they said Y?," not to change the interviewer's views, but to elucidate them more fully and understand the criteria that underlay interviewers' judgments. We also discussed possible questions that were not in the mock interview, including what is typically considered the hardest question of all: What is your biggest weakness? We had a particularly lively discussion about that question.

At some point, the HR folk let me in on a bit of a trade secret. HR professionals, when conducting employment interviews, are trained to ask questions so that they could put examples from the applicant's experience into a STAR format: Situation, Task, Actions, and Result. They wanted a description of the initial situation that the applicant had faced (place, people, etc.), the task that the applicant needed to perform, the actions that were taken, and the results of the action. This framework provided a coherent story – an elaborated answer – that I was constantly told is what interviewers wanted from the young people, but often did not get. We decided to train the young people in the STAR format. We could not realistically ask these HS students to give "elaborated answers," but we could teach them a structure that would enable them to provide detailed responses to the interviewer. I did not, however, think that STAR would work for these young people, especially the distinction between situation and task. So I came up with an alternative that I thought would be more accessible to this group of adolescents: CAR, which stood for Camera, Action, Results. The "camera" part of the framework involved imagining that they were taking a picture of the situation, who is there, what they are doing, and what the interviewee needs to do. The CAR framework was at the heart of our program as it could be adopted to answer the majority of questions that the interviewer might ask. I will describe shortly how we taught it.

CAR, however, was not the only important element in our program. It was also important to deal with the nonverbal aspects of the encounter. It was clear that in addition to evaluating the applicant's ability to do the tasks that the job required, the interviewer was concerned with whether the applicant's personality would fit with the culture of the workplace. In our situation, with a mock job, there was not a specific company culture to fit with, so this dimension basically boiled down to whether the applicant was someone you would want to work with, have on your team, and be comfortable interacting with in informal, workplace social situations. We could not change anyone's personality overnight, but we could help those young people who did poorly because they misunderstood what was expected of them in a job interview. Teaching them the culture of the employment interview involved guiding them in how to show their personality to best advantage and giving them tools to help them cope with the anxiety that the interview could provoke.

SOME BASICS OF THE CURRICULUM

We developed a five-session curriculum, expanded to six sessions at the request of some of the teachers who served as instructors for the program. Each session lasted a class period (approximately forty-five minutes) and the sessions were typically spread out over a two-week period. Although the school system initially suggested that my team and I deliver the curriculum ourselves, such an approach was ill-suited for providing the model for any scale-up. Instead, the students' main vocational teacher – recall that these programs were all in Career and Technical Education – delivered the program. The vocational tracks (some of which were in career academies) included health sciences, business/finance, culinary, and graphic arts. The program was implemented in three neighborhood high schools and in one vocational school. All of the students were juniors and they were in the second year of a three-year vocational program.

We typically provided one session of training, or professional development, to the teacher prior to the onset of the program. We observed each program session and provided an additional session of professional development midway through the curriculum.[2] The training emphasized role playing from both the mock job interview and the curriculum. The curriculum had an instructor's handbook, with approximately six pages for each session (double-spaced). We went over each section of each lesson with the teacher. The students had a sixteen-page Interview Skills Handbook that they used during the curriculum and were expected to keep as a reference for future interviews.[3]

The curriculum was preceded by a mock job interview for each student, administered by a paid HR interviewer (some HR professionals declined to receive payment and provided their services pro bono). The curriculum was also followed by a mock job interview, administered by an HR professional who was different from the person who had done the preinterviews. The postprogram interview was used in part for evaluation purposes and in part to motivate students to engage fully in the program so that they could do well in the upcoming second interview.

In what follows, I present the basic principles used in the program to help high school aged youth do well in job interviews. There were three major foci of our effort:

- Effectively communicating job-related skills and experiences
- Improving nonverbal skills
- Dealing with motivational questions

---

[2] This is in accord with findings by Berman and McLaughlin (1978), who conducted a classic, large-scale implementation study of school reform. They found that it was important to give ongoing training and not just preimplementation training. The additional session during implementation facilitates effectively addressing issues that come up as the teacher gained familiarity with the material. This approach enabled us as well to incorporate material that an individual teacher had effectively introduced, which often involved a particular phrase that the students appeared to respond well to (e.g., "give the details"). It also facilitated deleting material that had not worked well.

[3] We were told by some instructors, with wonderment, that none of their students had lost their notebook, which could be considered an unobtrusive measure of student interest.

Initial evaluation data are then presented from the pre- and post-mock job interviews conducted by the HR professionals. Drawing as well on our implementation of the program in an ASM apprenticeship, we consider some of the issues that would be involved in scaling up the program in varied settings.

In the process of teaching the students how to do well in job interviews, we also learned much from them. In particular, we learned that they had additional misconceptions about the interview that negatively impacted their performance. Surfacing these additional misconceptions enabled us to address them and strengthen the curriculum. We shall present these misconceptions in each of the following sections.

HOW TO COMMUNICATE JOB-RELATED SKILLS AND EXPERIENCES EFFECTIVELY

We were not sure what to expect when we had our initial professional development workshop with the vocational teachers. Would they be interested in what we offered or would they not believe in its potential value? We were gratified to learn from the outset that the teachers looked forward to getting training in this area and very much believed that their students needed work on these skills. The teachers uniformly believed that their students did not know how to "sell themselves," that they needed to learn how to more effectively communicate their skills to potential interviewers, whether for internships or jobs.

From the ASM2009 evaluation, we knew that many students did not believe that they had experiences and skills that would be valued in the workplace. As we worked with these vocational classes, we learned that if anything we had underestimated the extent of the problem. Even though in all of the different vocational tracks the students were learning a host of technical skills, they often did not think that they had any skills that employers would value. For example, take the students who were in the health sciences track. When the teacher held up an x-ray film for my analysis, in a sad attempt to hide my ignorance, I said something to the effect of "Well ... very interesting." The students, on the other hand, could point to the specific part of the x-ray image that revealed evidence of a broken bone. They could also take someone's blood pressure and do all sorts of other medical tasks many laypersons cannot do. But they didn't consider these to be work skills. Why? They would say "That's just school." Because it was learned and performed in school, they considered it to be schoolwork only. They did not believe that employers would be interested in what they learned or did in school.

In addressing this issue, we did not engage them in a debate or ponder abstract epistemological questions. Our curriculum was structured more as a series of workshops. We told them what business folk would consider skills and had them practice identifying skills, in part from written material we provided. The students then role played with their teachers how to identify their skill set when asked during an employment interview. Role play in response to simulated job interview questions was one of the keys to our program.

In responding to an interviewer prompt, we emphasized that the students had to "Prove It!" They needed to give an example of when they had used certain skills or behaved in a certain manner. They could not just say, "I have good communication skills" or "I am hardworking." Their answer had to "give the details" that would "prove it" to a curious interviewer who would not be convinced by abstract assertions of ability. Figure 6.1 presents a handout that we used in this part of the curriculum.

We spent a considerable amount of time teaching youth how to answer behavioral questions ("Tell me about a time when ...") using the CAR technique (Camera–Action–Results). We also taught them how to adapt the CAR technique to a variety of other types of queries, such as situational questions (e.g., "What would you do if ...") or those that on the surface appeared to require only a yes/no response (e.g., "Are you a leader?"). Figure 6.2 presents a handout we provided students to illustrate the CAR technique.

These workshops included whole-class discussions with different student volunteers. Hearing different students answer the identical job interview query would often prompt the other students to think of experiences they hadn't previously considered (e.g., in sports) that they could draw on in their own response. The teacher would then guide the class to provide feedback on the offered response using the following rubric:

- Did the student answer the question?
- Did the student give the details for the "Camera"? Ask for a volunteer to identify the "Camera" component of the response.
- Did the student give the details for two or more "Actions"? Ask for a volunteer to identify the "Actions" component of the response.
- Did the student give the details for the "Results"? Ask for a volunteer to identify the "Results" component of the response.

PROVE IT!

➢ **Use examples.** Don't just *tell* the interviewer you have important skills and qualities. PROVE IT by using examples from school, home, work, and after-school activities to demonstrate valuable job skills like leadership, teamwork, problem solving, and organization.

➢ **Give the details.** Share enough information to allow the interviewer to understand what you're talking about. Use the CAR technique (Lesson Two) to keep your response organized and easy to follow.

➢ **Relate to the job.** The purpose of each question is for the interviewer to decide whether you are right for a specific job. Help the interviewer picture you in the position. Think hard about the job responsibilities, choose your examples carefully, and explain to the interviewer how the experience has prepared you for this type of work.

FIGURE 6.1. Prove It handout.

By asking the class whether the student had actually answered the question, we encouraged students to focus on what they needed to address and not to get sidetracked in their answer. The other prompts made sure that the students gave the kind of elaborated answer that the HR interviewers would want. If the "results" did not include a positive outcome, students were instructed to emphasize what they had learned from the experience that they would apply in the future.

Were we giving the students "canned" answers to give to interviewers? We think not. Having worked with HR professionals for some time, we were acutely aware of their aversion to canned answers. They seemed to us always to be on the lookout for them and to downgrade an applicant when they thought they were being provided with an answer that the applicant

Camera – Take a mental picture of the situation and describe it to the interviewer. What's going on? Who's involved? What needs to be done?

Actions – What did you do and why? Try to give two good examples of actions you took.

Results – What was the outcome of the situation? Most importantly, what did you learn?

FIGURE 6.2. CAR handout.

had been taught. Instead, what we gave young people was a structure in which to deliver their responses, how they should talk about their experiences and skills, as well as information as to the kinds of experiences that would count as work experience.

IMPROVING NONVERBAL SKILLS

We would talk with the HR interviewers after they had completed the initial, preimplementation mock job interviews. In one class, the interviewer emphasized that although the students seemed smart and had learned a great deal in their classes, she had not judged them to be hirable because they were too "stiff" and interpersonally awkward. They did not seem like the type of person you would enjoy working with or chatting with at the water cooler.

In this (and related) instances, we found another youth misconception had taken hold. The students considered the interview to be a quiz in which they were to provide the correct answer as quickly and as briefly as possible. This put them on the spot and it was easy to understand how they might wind up tense as a result. We knew from observing interactions during class that many of these young people had good social skills that they had not used in the interview setting.

To provide an alternative framing that would put them more at ease, we emphasized that, from the interviewer's perspective, this was a "conversation, not a quiz." Yes, the interviewer was an authority figure, but he or she wanted to have a conversation with you. We talked about how they should "smile ... and relax," and make eye contact with the interviewer. And we had them practice introducing themselves and shaking hands (and shaking hands the same way with a female interviewer as for a male interviewer). Interviews were to be concluded with a smile, firm handshake, and brief remark.

DEALING WITH MOTIVATIONAL QUESTIONS

One of the first questions likely to arise in a job interview regards the reasons why an applicant is interested in the job. The interviewer will give preference to candidates who really want that particular job and have good reasons for being motivated. Working as we were with students in a particular vocational track, we had the students "apply" for a summer job in that particular vocational area. We encouraged them to begin by indicating what led them to become interested in the field in the first place. Many of the students had interesting personal histories that they could draw on; for example, in the health sciences track, many of them told of caring for family members or relatives with severe medical problems or physical disorders. We also advised them to indicate that they had made a three-year commitment to that vocational area, and they were now in their second year (as juniors), which indicated seriousness and dependability. Finally, we had the students talk about their future plans and how this job would contribute to their long-range goals (even if their long-term goals included a career in a different occupational area).

Another area of the job interview involves the young person asking questions about the job. This will be taken as an indication of interest and seriousness about the job, as well as interest in learning. Here, again, we encountered an important youth misconception. Many of the young people were adverse, or reluctant, to ask the interviewer any questions because they assumed that to do so would be taken as a sign of rudeness or disrespect. After all, they thought, asking the interviewer questions about the job seemed to suggest that the interviewer hadn't done his or her job well. So we reframed this, telling them that interviewers wanted them to ask questions, to demonstrate interest, and that this was part of the interview being a conversation. Part of one session was devoted to discussing possible questions and having students role play by asking questions of the teacher (who played the job interviewer).

The program, overall, gives young people the wide range of skills needed for employment interviews. In their research with employers, economists Philip Moss and Chris Tilly quoted a retail store manager who hired minority youth (high school graduates), but who complained vociferously that they were not well prepared for the hiring interview:

> "They've not been trained in high school. They just don't seem to know how to apply for a job. They don't know how to dress. They simply answer questions yes and no. They don't ask about the job. They don't seem interested. They don't show up on a timely basis. That just seems like a bad way to apply for a job."[4]

This program addresses the complaints of this manager – and, presumably, those of others. And many other employers, unlike this manager, will not hire young people who do not do well in the job interview.

INITIAL EVALUATION FINDINGS

The findings from the initial evaluation of the program were quite positive. We compared interviewers' precurriculum rating of whether they would hire the young person for a permanent job with postcurriculum ratings. This involved seventy students across five classes. The hiring rate effectively doubled from pre- (27 percent) to post- (53 percent), a finding that was statistically significant ($t = 3.42$, $p < .01$). This is a substantial increase.[5] In examining scores for each class, it appeared that there was a meaningful increase for four of the five classes. The one class that did not demonstrate improvement was an honors class, with strict enrollment requirements, which had a high hiring rate at the preassessment.

We also paid particular attention to the class in the worst school. That school had an average absence rate of eleven weeks per academic year. We were warned beforehand by their teacher and an administrator to expect that many students would not enter the class on time; indeed, a number

---

[4] Moss & Tilly (2001), p. 233.
[5] Effect size, $g = .55$ on the dichotomous variable of being hired or not hired; .66 on the continuous 1–5 scale.

of students made their way into the class well into the session. Even in this class, however, the hiring rate went from 17 percent before the curriculum to 50 percent postcurriculum. As these students are among the most difficult to reach, this result is heartening.[6]

Because there was no control group for this evaluation, we cannot be certain that it was our program that produced this change. For example, repeated participation in the interview may have led to improved performance. So although these results are promising, they need to be considered with caution.

Let us examine the other ratings that the HR interviewers made to help us understand why the program appeared to succeed. In looking at the "A" ratings in Table 6.1 (those that refer to a specific interview question), we can see statistically significant effects on six of the thirteen items, all of which indicate a positive impact for the program. The strongest effects were for the first question (1A), in which students were asked why they applied for this specific job, and for question 11A, which asked them how this job might contribute to their life in the next few years. Both of these areas, which tap the applicant's motivation, were covered in our curriculum in the next-to-last session. It is possible that students were able to make better use of material covered later in the curriculum as they had gained familiarity with the broader material and frameworks we were using. Another reason might be that those two questions were specifically addressed during a session. In general, we were loath to train youth on specific questions, because interviews vary; instead, we sought to provide them with a host of questions, culled from several interview sources, so that they would be well prepared for varied questions in a specific domain. We made an exception for these two questions, especially the first one – Why did you apply for this job? – because it is likely to come up in almost every interview.

In terms of the "B" items, which tapped more general impressions of the interviewee, there were statistically significant effects on five of the twelve items (excluding the two hiring measures), and again all indicated a

---

[6] We should point out that only six students in this class completed both the pre- and postassessments, and they might constitute a biased sample. Furthermore, in a focus group after the postassessment, some of the students indicated that my presence (fifty-ish white man), along with that of an African American graduate student (thirty-something woman), may have inhibited the class; this was the only class where this appeared to be an issue. It is possible that without our presence, the students might have learned more, which could have resulted in better scores and more students who participated in the final assessment.

TABLE 6.1 *Changes in mean ratings on the Northwestern Mock Job Interview (N = 70)*

	Pre- M (SD)	Post- M (SD)	t-ratio	p-value
1A – Why applied	3.19 (0.94)	3.67 (0.83)	−3.79	.001
2A – What experiences do you have	3.89 (1.00)	3.76 (0.94)	0.94	.349
3A – Recent goal	3.71 (1.28)	3.94 (1.09)	−1.50	.139
4A – Working with others	3.96 (1.08)	4.30 (0.87)	−2.57	.012
5A – Complete a project by deadline	3.96 (0.96)	4.24 (0.88)	−2.27	.026
6A – Dealing with angry person	3.77 (1.21)	3.96 (1.21)	−1.06	.293
7A – Disagree with supervisor	4.29 (1.14)	4.74 (0.63)	−3.40	.001
8A – Stay late to cover shifts	4.67 (0.70)	4.71 (0.59)	−0.37	.713
9A – Special event conflict	4.70 (0.67)	4.66 (0.66)	0.42	.678
10A – Trouble with photocopier	4.44 (0.86)	4.60 (0.69)	−1.56	.124
11A – How job contributes to future	3.60 (1.17)	4.11 (0.99)	−3.45	.001
12A – Questions about job	3.34 (1.59)	3.91 (1.25)	−2.49	.015
13A – What else about you	3.41 (0.69)	3.47 (0.72)	−0.49	.626
1B – Initial impression	3.67 (0.68)	3.64 (0.80)	0.28	.780
2B – Dress and appearance	3.60 (1.00)	3.91 (0.94)	−2.17	.033
3B – Eye contact	4.20 (0.77)	4.49 (0.63)	−2.44	.017
4B – Positive attitude	4.17 (.76)	4.34 (0.72)	−1.65	.103
5B – Body language	4.09 (0.61)	4.14 (0.62)	−0.63	.531
6B – Confidence	3.47 (1.11)	3.93 (0.87)	−3.32	.001
7B – Paid attention	4.30 (0.69)	4.50 (0.61)	−1.91	.061
8B – Communication	3.01 (0.99)	3.54 (0.85)	−4.35	.001
9B – Maturity	3.81 (0.91)	4.20 (0.88)	−2.85	.006
10B – Application completion	2.82 (0.98)	3.20 (1.39)	−1.69	.098
11B – Prior experience	3.45 (0.93)	3.51 (0.89)	−0.45	.654
12B – Response to feedback	4.50 (0.64)	4.37 (0.62)	1.10	.278

positive treatment impact. The strongest effects were for three items: clear communication (B8), confidence (B6), and maturity (B9).

These quantitative findings are consistent with our own judgments when we viewed videos of the pre- and postinterviews. For the ASM2009 evaluation, which involved many more youth, we were logistically unable to videotape the interviews. But for this new program, with fewer youth, we were able to do this. We studied those videos before conducting the statistical analyses, so the overlap (convergent validity) is noteworthy.

Our observations revealed that in the postimplementation mock job interviews, compared to the preimplementation interviews, students focused more clearly on the question asked by the interviewer and rambled less, used better examples to highlight their skills effectively, and appeared more thoughtful and reflective. Indeed, using the HR terminology, the students gave much more elaborated answers. In terms of nonverbal behavior, students were less nervous and fidgety, less stiff, more relaxed and easygoing, smiling extensively. This is quite consistent with the interviewer ratings of gains in communication skills and confidence. As the young people demonstrated greater ease and comfort talking with adults, and addressed work issues more insightfully, it is not surprising that they were rated as more mature.

We compiled video clips of several students who had improved on interviewer ratings from pre- to postinterview. We juxtaposed their responses to specific questions, first showing the pre- answer and then the post- answer to each of several questions. We showed the video to the top administrator in Career and Technical Education and she concurred with our analysis. This direct viewing of the qualitative data made an impression on her and she became a stronger advocate of our program. Moreover, speaking as someone who knows what it's like to be a parent of two teens, I would imagine that most parents would be quite pleased if their own child demonstrated these types of gains over such a short period.

We interviewed several of the teachers who had implemented the program to assess their reactions. Uniformly, the teachers indicated that the curriculum had met their expectations and had been of benefit. One teacher said that

> *I got something valuable because I'm already teaching interview skills but never put things in terms of having them prove it. That was a really big deal for me ... being able to explain exactly how to do it. I really liked that part.*

Another teacher said that the curriculum did a "wonderful job" of meeting the needs of the students because "it really filled a gap." We asked her what she meant by a gap. She explained that last year the students took part in an interview preparation program called Soft Skills but she did not seem very impressed with the program. She said the Northwestern interview skills curriculum is "very specific" in teaching the skills and techniques to prepare students for interviews. A third teacher reported that the curriculum met the needs of his students in that "it's the next step" in preparing them for real job interviews. The interviews that they had been exposed to in the past introduced students to the "basics," but the Northwestern program provided greater "focus" and "structure" that goes beyond what the students already received.

IMPLEMENTATION IN AFTER SCHOOL MATTERS

After the implementations in Chicago Public Schools, we asked ASM whether they would be interested in our delivering a modified version of the curriculum to one of their apprenticeships. They readily agreed and we implemented the program in a summer dance apprenticeship run by experienced instructors.

There were several modifications to the program that we wanted to test out in ASM. First, we wanted to see how well the program worked in an after-school program setting. A number of modifications were made, especially removing material focusing on a particular vocational track and opening up the types of job to which students might apply. Second, we wanted to see how well the program could be implemented if a student's school teacher or ASM instructor did not deliver the material, so a member of our staff taught the curriculum. Although many ASM instructors could teach the program, some of them would not want to. We thought that ASM supervisors would enjoy and do a good job at delivering the program, so one of them observed several of our program sessions. Third, we wanted to gain some idea of how well the program might work in the absence of any mock job interviews. When we initially talked about our research with the top Chicago Public Schools administrator, she proclaimed that every high school student ought to have the experience of a mock job interview as part of their education. Since that time, however, she (and her successors) had spent untold hours in meetings to trim millions of dollars from the budget. In a time of dire finances, we wondered how realistic it might ever be to have HR professionals on staff just to provide mock job interviews. In 2014 at Northwestern University, a full-time, beginning HR professional would have a salary of $40,000–50,000, plus benefits. A school system in a major city would require many interviewers, driving up implementation costs (and these would be recurring costs). In the absence of paid HR professionals, the cost of the program is otherwise minimal, which is a strong selling point.

A twenty-something female member of our staff delivered the program and quickly established a good rapport with the apprentices. She also played the role of a job interviewer in our many role plays. Modification of the material to reflect the backgrounds and interests of these young people was easily accomplished.

Were there differences in the quality of youth responses during program activities in this implementation versus those that had been preceded by the mock job interview? We were not able to discern any. The young people seemed just as actively involved and appeared to learn the material at a similar rate and level of quality. However, we did not formally evaluate this, so we should say that the results were promising rather than definitive.

Our experience in implementing the program in ASM suggests that the content of the program could be adapted easily to the after-school setting. The young people in the dance program seemed to enjoy and learn from the workshops (curriculum) we provided. Within ASM itself, we thought that the sessions could be led by ASM supervisors, who tended to have a stronger background and interest in youthwork than a number of the instructors. After-school workers would probably need more ongoing supervision in implementing the material than high school teachers, who generally have a greater familiarity with structured educational programs.

A CONCEPTUAL AND POLICY CODA

Young people need to learn how to communicate effectively in job interviews, and this involves both verbal and nonverbal behavior. One way of thinking about this is to recognize that youth need to learn the discourse of those interviews. Taking a sociolinguistic approach, James Gee argued that to be accepted in other settings, it is necessary to become fluent in the discourse of those worlds:

> Discourses are ways of being in the world, or forms of life which integrate words, acts, values, beliefs, attitudes, and social identities, as well as gestures, glances, body positions, and clothes. A Discourse is a sort of identity kit which comes complete with the appropriate costume and instructions on how to act, talk, and often write, so as to take on a particular social role that others will recognize.[7]

This appears to capture quite well what our HR interviewers required and what our curriculum was designed to achieve.

On a policy level, it is important to appreciate that we were training young people in the discourse needed to enter what is often referred to as the primary labor market. Social scientists distinguish between jobs

---

[7] Gee (1996), p. 127.

in the primary labor market and those in the secondary labor market.[8] Primary labor market jobs tend to be stable, with good pay, opportunities for advancement, and employee benefits (e.g., health insurance). Those in the secondary labor market are often referred to as dead-end jobs, unstable, poorly paid, and without benefits or career potential. In the last chapter, it was clear that the HR professionals considered a number of the youth they had interviewed to have management potential. The HR professionals themselves came from primary labor market firms and in their curriculum consultation sought to help us develop the interview skills – and, more fully, the discourse – that would enable youth to obtain jobs in that sector. This is a distinctive feature of our effort, as not all training programs for adolescents seek to provide to provide the tools necessary for primary sector jobs.

FUTURE DIRECTIONS

This new program is not the first to offer training in job interview skills. But most programs provide only a rudimentary introduction. This is clear from reading program reports, and the teachers we worked with confirmed that this was their experience. By implication, program developers do not consider this an important area in need of sustained attention. Our own experience suggests otherwise. Many young people have a host of misconceptions about the interview that can lead them to underperform. When provided with structured training that addresses those misconceptions and teaches them important communication skills, their mock hiring rate doubled.

Developmentally, we taught youth a type of transfer or bridging skill. Skills of this sort enable a young person to bring to a new environment experiences and skills that were acquired in prior environments.[9] Job interviewers look to see whether young people have the types of skills that can cross this bridge and bring value to the workplace. They judge whether the young person is ready to make the developmental transition from school to work. It is crucial for young people to demonstrate these skills in job interviews.[10]

---

[8] This is the theory of labor market segmentation (e.g., Berger & Piore, 1980; Doeringer & Piore, 1971; Emmenegger et al., 2012).

[9] National Research Council (2012).

[10] This formulation is influenced by developmental psychologist Uri Bronfenbrenner's work on the ecology of human development (his 1979 book is the classic work). In Bronfenbrenner's terms, this type of transfer or bridging skill invokes the mesosystem, or connections between two different microsystems (such as work and school). The young person seeks, for example, to get an HR professional in the work microsystem that she hopes to enter to become aware of what the student has done at school and to see that

The development of job interview skills can and should be expanded so that it becomes an integral part of what students learn in school. The material we presented can be infused into academic topics and lesson plans. For example, whenever a course topic is completed, the students could practice how they would talk about the new material they have learned in a job interview. This ongoing attention would strengthen the real-world benefit of the material, as well as the students' communication skills.

Linking academic content to real-world benefits in this manner might enhance student's motivation to learn the academic material. Although we explored how interview training could be implemented in career and technical education, it could also be utilized in more traditional academic arenas. Just as the program seemed to work well with a dance apprenticeship in ASM, it would seem well suited to any academic area that made use of student teams. Teamwork is employed in several standard academic areas (e.g., science) and teamwork skills are a priority in today's contemporary workforce. This would not involve substituting vocational material for academic learning, but rather demonstrating that the ways in which students learned the academic material could be appreciated by employers.

It should be clear that much further research is needed. More evaluation studies need to be conducted that include control groups and follow-up. The nature and extent of student misconceptions about job interviews, and adult jobs more generally, needs explication. Given the important role that HR professionals play as gatekeepers for entry into the workforce, their attitudes and beliefs need to be better understood.

Job interview training has been underappreciated. The development of skills in this area is a crucial, final step in making sure that experiences and skills can be successfully communicated. If you don't do well in a job interview, you likely won't get the job even if your hard skills are superior. This is true for everyone. But job interview skills are especially important to teenagers from underprivileged backgrounds so that they can enter the work world in the first place.

the skills demonstrated at school correspond to important responsibilities in the work position for which she is interviewing. Bronfenbrenner was focused on the effects of connections between environments on a child (the mesosystem in this instance); my intent is to see how such an analytic framework speaks to the kind of skills that would be useful for youth to develop.

7

Guidelines for the Future

Integrating youth into the workforce is a challenge for every society. In much of Western Europe, most notably in Germany, the focus is on workplace-based apprenticeship systems. In the United States, the emphasis historically has been on school-based training in vocational tracks. The US system has come under attack from both the political right and left for slotting low-income youth at an early age into tracks that lead to less remunerative occupations.

The problem of youth workforce development is especially severe among minority youth. Their official unemployment rate is typically nearly double that of majority youth. As is well known, low-income minority youth suffer broadly from poor resources in their schools and communities, and not just from a lack of work opportunities.

The potential of after-school programs to step into this gap is intriguing. These programs have existed for well over 100 years, yet only recently have they targeted high school aged youth with job-related programs.[1] Youth who participate in after-school programs can be enrolled in college preparatory tracks in high school, so the programs are able to sidestep one of the most trenchant criticisms of academically based vocational programs: that they steer youth away from college.

In this context, it was a rare and welcome opportunity to be able to conduct a random assignment, experimental evaluation of After School Matters, widely considered the flagship program of those that provide high school youth with job-oriented programming. The evaluation focused on After School Matters as it operated during the time of our research (2006–2009), hence our continual reference to it as ASM2009. As it turned out, contrary to what had been predicted by ASM2009 before the study,

---

[1] Halpern (2003) provides some history of the development of these programs.

most of the youth in the control group (91 percent) were in an alternative, organized after-school activity (e.g., sports, arts) and thus constituted an alternative treatment group, which was a higher bar for ASM2009 than if it were being compared to a no-treatment group. Almost all youth in the evaluation (99 percent) were either African American or Hispanic.

The major methodological innovation of the research was in the development and use of a mock job interview for high-school students. The interview was developed in collaboration with senior human resource (HR) professionals and was administered by experienced HR professionals. A total of twenty-eight HR professionals participated in this effort. We utilized HR professionals to maximize the external credibility of the mock job findings, especially to those in the business and policy worlds. The extensive qualitative component of the research enabled us to open up the "black box" of what went on inside the thirteen ASM2009 apprenticeships. Findings from these mixed methods complemented and supported each other.

The evaluation of ASM2009, the first of the two new program directions we studied, yielded results that both did and did not support the promise of ASM2009's approach to youth workforce development. On the positive side, we saw that ASM2009 youth in each of the apprenticeships were able to develop hard skills particular to the field of the apprenticeship. Soft skills, which would be useful in a variety of jobs, were also developed, even if they were often not an explicit focus of the instructors. Many of the final products or performances were engaging and of good quality. Several of the instructors were excellent.

Unfortunately, the hiring rates for ASM2009 youth in the mock job interview were not significantly different statistically from those of youth in the control group. ASM2009 avoided the severe implementation problems that can plague programs in evaluation studies (e.g., long stretches in which they do not operate, fundamental deviations from the program model), but there were more implementation difficulties than had been anticipated. After all, we (ASM2009 and the research team) had purposefully selected what we presumed to be among the better apprenticeships for this research. We knew this would entail limitations in terms of our ability to generalize the findings, but wanted to give ASM2009 its "best chance" to demonstrate impact by minimizing implementation variation and instead focus on the utility of the project-based model when it is implemented well.

By using our qualitative data, we were able to generate plausible hypotheses about why ASM2009 youth did not do better on the mock job interview. A strength of this approach is that we were able to ground our qualitative analysis in the quantitative data from the interview; that is, we selected apprenticeships based on their hiring data relative to their control group and thus could meaningfully relate the process data to outcome data obtained independently. It would have been even better had we been able to conduct such implementation or process analyses with control group programs as well, but that was not possible.

The first insight was that youth soft skills – such as problem solving, communication, teamwork, and leadership–were important to hiring decisions and many ASM2009 apprenticeships did not do a good job of teaching those skills. The reasons for this varied. Too many instructors were weak themselves in this area and thus not well equipped to teach them to youth; indeed, they sometimes modeled very poor skills in this area. Other instructors simply did not make it a point of emphasis.

The second insight, which we owe to the HR interviewers (Chapter 5), was that many youth did not recognize the job skills that they had and did not communicate them effectively in the interview. This was true of both ASM2009 and control group youth. Thus, even if, let us say, ASM2009 apprenticeships provided superior hard skills than did the control group programs (which we do not know), the failure to teach those job recognition and interview skills means that they would not be demonstrated in the mock job interview. ASM2009 did not do enough to make the job skills that they did teach *marketable*, although this was one of the program's top goals. Had ASM2009 apprenticeships done a better job of teaching soft skills, and a better job of teaching their youth to recognize and communicate their hard and soft job skills, then ASM2009 might well have been able to demonstrate superiority to the range of existing program alternatives in developing marketable job skills. The available evidence, however, indicates that ASM2009 was not a superior youth workforce development program.

Growing organically out of the HR debriefings, the second new program direction we studied involved the development and implementation of an initiative to teach high school youth the job recognition and communication skills that they needed (Chapter 6). The pre–post mock hiring data from the HR interviewers suggest that we were able to greatly improve the hiring rates, and underlying skills, of the young people who participated in this brief, six-session program. This effort can be achieved relatively quickly and at modest cost. However, we did not have a control group for this evaluation, so the conclusions are tentative.

We now want to address what we learned from these studies in an integrative manner. Our objective in doing so is to use this new knowledge to improve youth workforce development efforts. Our intent is not to suggest a comprehensive model because we do not have data that address everything that would need to be included in such a model. We want to base our recommendations on the data we do have and to highlight important system elements that require careful attention. I hope that keeping this next section brief and focused will maximize its potential use by programs as well as the social policy community.

JOB HIRING AS THE ANCHOR POINT

It is essential to have a clear idea of the outcomes that are to be achieved. If we wish to increase the number of minority youth who obtain paid employment, then the hiring rate is the critical variable.[2] As discussed in Chapter 2, hiring decisions are typically made in employment interviews. Accordingly, the objective should be to increase positive hiring rates in employment interviews. This is the desired endpoint and we should take care to keep our eye on the prize.[3]

One of the weaknesses of ASM2009, and many related policies and programs, is that there was an overly fuzzy and vague notion of the endpoint. For ASM2009, it was the ill-defined "marketable job skills." When we began our work with them, these skills were mostly thought of as hard skills and as employment, or entry into a college major, that mapped specifically unto the hard skills taught in the apprenticeship. This was despite the fact that many youth, even in high school vocational programs, will seek and gain employment in unrelated fields.[4] This is especially true in the arts, in which ASM2009 had many apprenticeships, but in which there are regrettably few employment possibilities.

For many youth programs, particularly those involving high school youth, an actual employment interview and hiring decision is off in the future, too distal an outcome. Instead, such programs could reasonably use hiring decisions in a mock job interview as the key outcome. Presumably, mock job hiring decisions will predict performance in a real job interview, although that remains to be established in empirical research.

---

[2] Ratings made during job interviews have been empirically linked to work productivity, such as supervisor evaluations (see Chapter 2, footnote 2).

[3] Heifetz (1994), in one of his many excellent books on leadership in the nonprofit sector, emphasizes the need of leaders to keep their "eye on the prize."

[4] Stone & Lewis (2012). There is considerable movement among youth to obtain employment outside of the area of training in the German apprenticeship system as well (Hamilton, 1990).

MAIN PROGRAM IMPLICATIONS

Assuming, then, that we are seeking to enhance the employment prospects of low-income, minority youth who are still in high school, what type of program would best prepare them for doing well in a mock job interview? In asking the question in this way, I am drawing on work on backward mapping in the policy area.[5] In adapting this approach, one seeks to determine, first, the type of program that best increases the likelihood of positive mock hiring, which we can call Program A. Then, successively, our task is to identify the types of programs (and policies) that provide the strongest foundation for benefitting from Program A. We will only back up a few steps in this chapter, because our research best addresses those specific steps. This is the strength of the research that was conducted and it addresses a serious gap in our knowledge.

It should be noted that the logic of the presentation differs in this section from what we have followed in the earlier part of the book. In the prior chapters, we followed a historical logic, presenting ASM2009 before the interview training, because that is the sequence in which the programs were both developed and evaluated. In a backward mapping approach, however, the logic is determined by the proximity of the intervention to achieving the outcome (hiring, in this instance). For the problem of minority youth employment, this focuses attention on ways of thinking about the issue that have previously not received sufficient consideration.

Job Interview Training

It seems reasonable to hypothesize that the program most immediately and directly related to mock hiring decisions (Program A) would be one that focuses on job interview skills (see Figure 7.1). We have seen that there are a number of highly specific skills and attitudes to teach for young people to become competent in the discourse expected in that setting. Moreover, our findings from the HR debriefings indicate that many youth lack these skills. Indeed, youth have a number of misconceptions that, if not addressed, will undermine their performance. Our experience suggests that these misconceptions need to be addressed repeatedly and that the skills need to be practiced in role plays on multiple occasions with diverse prompts. The work that is required is of sufficient depth that a program is required, whether

---

[5] See, in particular, Elmore (1979/1980, 1985). Munoz (2005) provides a brief summary of the approach.

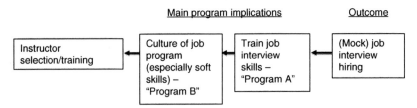

FIGURE 7.1. Main program recommendations from a backward-mapping approach.

it be a stand-alone program or integrated with a more comprehensive job training program (which is what we did with the vocational classes in Chicago Public Schools and with the dance apprenticeship in ASM).

We presented in Chapter 6 a promising program to teach job interview skills to high school youth. We do not yet have enough evaluation data to come to a summative conclusion about the merit of the program we developed, the conditions and groups for which it works best, and so on. There are alternative programs that already exist. More such programs could be developed and evaluated.

Hard and Soft Skill Training

The next step, in working backwards, is to consider the type of program that will best prepare high school youth to take advantage of a job interview program. Let us designate as Program B that program that best prepares youth for the job interview program (Program A).

Our analysis of the two best-hire apprenticeship programs in Chapter 3 suggests that Program B should be grounded, in part, in basic communication skills applicable to the workplace. The culture of the program needs to be such that young people develop a comfort level in discussing work-related issues with adults in authority positions. Youth need experience in providing an explicit rationale for why they did one thing rather than another at their site. They need to learn how to give and respond to feedback. Once they have these basic workplace communications skills, they will be better prepared to take advantage of the more specialized communication training related to job interviews.

It also is essential that youth have work experiences that they can talk about when they get to the job interview training. So Program B should provide important work-related experiences. Programs at this stage combine hard and soft skills. Youth need to develop hard skills and complete tasks that depend on the utilization of hard skills. At the same time, they need to learn to work hard and become committed to producing quality work. Problem-solving, teamwork, relationship building, and so on are incorporated as part of this effort.

Youth need to be taught explicitly to recognize that they are learning job skills in Program B. They need to understand that these are skills that are transferable to paid employment settings and will be valued by employers. This applies to both hard and soft skills. Youth must be taught to appreciate how Program B activities are aligned with those of various paid jobs.

The soft skills learned in Program B are vital to improving hiring rates. It is no doubt preferable that there be a close match between hard skills learned in a program and those required in a job. Nevertheless, many young people who obtain specific hard skills in Program B will seek jobs that involve a different hard skill set. It is also the case that employers often prefer to train new employees in the employer's own approach to hard skills. These factors limit the utility of hard skills learned in training programs. Soft skills, on the other hand, are generic to many employment situations and are highly valued in today's workforce. Training youth in soft skills is key to increasing their probability of finding a job. Youth are short changed when programs focus on hard skills at the expense of soft skills.

The importance of soft skills to employer hiring of young people is supported in Stephen Hamilton's study of German apprenticeships. It is to be recalled that the German apprenticeship system is often considered the gold standard for youth workforce development. As noted in Chapter 3, Hamilton found that employers emphasized *Arbeitstugende*, or worker virtues, in hiring. These worker virtues are similar to what I have referred to as soft skills. Hamilton concluded that these virtues were what youth needed to know on any job and their development was the most important outcome of apprenticeship training.[6] The fact that similar characteristics were found in both our study and the German apprenticeship system argues that soft skills are critical to improving hiring rates of minority youth.

In Chapters 3 and 4, we presented three programs that found ways to develop these skills. The youth in each of those programs had excellent hiring rates on the mock job interview. The organized team competition model, in particular, led to high levels of engagement and standards of work quality. A variety of tactics could be gleaned from the other two programs that should be considered by program leaders. Unfortunately, the overall authoritative mentoring model, although theoretically appealing to many,

---

[6] Hamilton (1990).

cannot be recommended in its entirety as it is likely to be too difficult to implement successfully.

These types of programs fit well into a positive youth development framework. The evaluation findings and our analyses address business concerns, but they fit just as easily into a developmental framework. By focusing on experiences and skills that lead to increased hiring, that increase the ability of young people to assume meaningful roles in the adult world, programs promote development in ways that are highly salient to young people and their families. SongScape, Elite Eats, and Youth View not only led to better hiring rates, but were also model youth development programs. Youth development and workforce development should proceed in tandem.

Staff Hiring

Backing up one more step, if teaching soft skills to youth is important, that suggests that staff should be hired who bring strong soft skills to the program (furthest left box in Figure 7.1). This was not a hiring priority for ASM2009 as they thought, mistakenly, that they were providing an appropriate level of training. The issue of selecting staff for hard versus soft skills, and related issues concerning staff training and supervision, are complex. We did not observe ASM2009's efforts in this area and thus cannot bring data to bear on the question. We do, however, want to note that this issue is critical to the success of youth workforce development and that the mock job hiring data indicated that the impact of ASM2009's hiring and training process was insufficient. This is an area in which research is very much needed.

It is in the three boxes on the right in Figure 7.1 that our findings are strongest. It is also those areas that most lack prior theory and research, so our contributions are distinctive and worth noting.

IMPLICATIONS FOR PRIVATE SECTOR HIRING

Corporations are not oriented toward seeking teen employees. Yet we found in this research that their own HR professionals judged that many of the minority high school youth they interviewed would make a positive contribution to the workplace and were hirable. In prior research with Stephanie Riger, presented in Chapter 5, we discussed how work supervisors valued the summer work of minority high school students and would have liked to have hired many of them for permanent positions. There are thus good reasons for firms to expand the positions they make available to these young people, especially in the summer when school is not in session.

From the perspective of students, having more private sector job opportunities would help youth appreciate how their experiences and skills in training programs transfer to real jobs. It would also likely enhance the motivation to acquire skills in training programs when they knew that such skills could help them get a summer job, for example, in the near future.

Here are three recommendations that flow from these prior research studies and that would enhance the value of the main program implications just presented.

1. Provide more summer job opportunities in the private sector for low-income high school youth.[7] Unpaid internships are also a possibility. It should be noted, though, that many of these youth were not familiar with the concept of an internship; firms would need to devote resources to insuring that youth interns not only had significant work assignments, but that they were repeatedly informed that what they were doing would be considered as work experience by future employers even though it was unpaid.[8]

2. Link summer jobs to post-high school employment. A number of firms employ college students in summer jobs and then offer the best candidates a position to start on graduation. Could not something similar be put in place for low-income, high school youth? Clearly, we are talking about different types of jobs than for college graduates, but the principle is the same. Conduct realistic interviews for the paid summer jobs. Put the youth through a trial, doing genuine work. Hire the ones who do excellent work and are recommended by their supervisors. These would be part-time jobs for youth who are taking college courses. If these are full-time jobs, then we would be talking of those youth who are not going on to college. We saw from a detailed look at school grades that many youth whom HR professionals would want to hire, with enthusiasm, had only modest grades, and a good job might provide a more realistic alternative than

---

[7] This book is especially concerned with minority youth. However, in the current era, it is likelier that new employment initiatives would be targeted at low-income youth rather than youth as defined by their race or ethnicity.

[8] There is also a legal question of whether interns should be paid. There would be some tension between not paying interns but telling them that what they were doing would be considered the equivalent of paid work.

trying, unsuccessfully, to get a college degree after a record of weak high school academic performance.

3. Eliminate the requirement of "six months experience" as needed for entry level positions as many youth will have experience, but it will not be from paid employment. This needlessly confuses and discourages youth and their families. Instead, note that "experience with these skills is required."

IMPLICATIONS FOR FEDERAL AND STATE POLICY

Federal and state policies could be developed to promote what I have referred to as the main program implications of this research. Such policies could also support the private sector hiring initiatives just sketched.

Federal and state policies could stipulate that the inclusion of these specified programs or program elements are necessary to receive, or be given high priority for, employment training or targeted education funding. The funding could be used for programs, research, or both. In addition, the main program implications could be included in developing new standards for employment training and education activities. These new policy targets would include the following:

- Include (mock) job interview training in workforce development, CTE (Career and Technical Education) tracks in schools, and non-CTE tracks in schools that target low-income youth. Job interview training would not substitute for academic content in non-CTE tracks, but would teach students how what they have learned in school would be valued by employers; this would fit most easily in subjects, such as science, that regularly make use of student teams and project-based learning.
- Infuse job interview training skills into the regular curriculum (e.g., after each curriculum unit has ended, practice how to present that unit's material to a job interviewer).
- Youth vocational and workforce development efforts, both in and out of school, should include a strong emphasis on the development of soft skills.
- Evaluate the effects of different types of instructor hires and instructor training on the quality of program implementation. Particular attention should be paid to efforts to identify the best profile of instructor hard and soft skills.

- Evaluate the implementation feasibility and utility of organized team competition on youth motivation and the quality of youth work.
- Place HR professionals in low-income schools to provide students with the experience of a mock job interview as part of their overall education.
- Utilize a mock job interview as an outcome measure in both formative and summative evaluation research.

Finally, the following government policy initiatives could support the private sector hiring sketched earlier:

- Strengthen private sector summer employment opportunities.
- Establish and evaluate private sector employments options that link successful summer job performance of low-income youth with continued employment. Employment would be part-time for those who enter college, full-time for those who do not go to college.

Youth workforce development policies and programs are complex. These suggestions do not amount to a comprehensive system. But they appear to be useful elements that would focus attention on important processes and outcomes especially relevant to young people.

Minority youth unemployment is a serious problem and needs to be addressed proactively with major efforts directed at high school students. Youth workforce development will not take place overnight. An understanding of how to bridge positive youth development with the needs of employers will be central to successful initiatives. Hard outcome measures, such as mock job interview results, need to be included to evaluate the success of those efforts and to learn how best to strengthen the programs.

Appendix 1

The Impact of After School Matters on Positive Youth Development, Academics, and Problem Behavior

This appendix presents results from a three-year, random assignment evaluation of After School Matters (ASM) as it operated during the years 2006–2009 (hereafter referred to as ASM2009). The major question addressed here is whether assignment to and participation in ASM2009 apprenticeships resulted in gains in positive youth development and academic performance, and in decreases in problem behavior. Findings regarding marketable job skills are, for the most part, reported in the chapters of this book, though they are integrated into parts of the discussion section of this appendix.

As with the other parts of the book, the appendix is written to be accessible not only to academics and researchers, but also to those in the policy and practice worlds. However, I think it fair to say that the appendix is written in a bit more of a detailed, academic style than the chapters in the book. At the same time, I have not included all possible information and have supplied only one table. Those who want an even more detailed account should consult our Technical Report on the evaluation, which can be downloaded for free from either Hirsch's faculty webpage or the website of the Wallace Foundation.[1]

BACKGROUND

Over the past few years, after-school programs have attracted a strong and growing constituency among both academic theorists and policymakers.

[1] Hirsch et al. (2011).

Appendix 1 is coauthored by Barton J. Hirsch, Larry V. Hedges, JulieAnn Stawicki, and Megan A. Mekinda.

Challenging activities and relationships with caring staff can lead to important developmental gains by increasing skills, instilling confidence, broadening cultural horizons, and promoting positive values.[2] Potential policy implications range from reducing youth crime during the high-risk 3–6 PM period to supporting school reform efforts and promoting workforce preparation and positive youth development.

Some reviewers have concluded that initial findings on the effectiveness of after-school programs are promising. Durlak, Weissberg, and Pachan completed a comprehensive meta-analysis on the effectiveness of after-school programs that is most relevant to our evaluation. Overall, they found an average positive effect size of approximately one-quarter of a standard deviation. The effect was larger for programs they defined as being highly structured, programs whose activities were sequenced, active, focused, and explicit. However other meta-analyses have employed different selection criteria, emphasized different outcomes, and yielded less favorable conclusions about program effectiveness.[3]

There are important methodological limitations to much research on after-school programs. Many studies failed to include pretest measures of outcomes and had no or poorly matched comparison groups.[4] There have been few randomized controlled trials. Randomization is the best procedure for guarding against selection effects in which youth more likely to improve over time are disproportionately located in the treatment group. In that event, it is impossible to sort out whether effects are due to selection (who got into the program) or the program itself (the experiences of youth while in the program).

Furthermore, the large majority of programs evaluated using randomized control group designs served elementary and middle school students, rather than high school students. The comparative paucity of studies on effects for high school students is not surprising as most after-school programs serve younger children. Although the forty largest national youth organizations reach approximately forty million youth, participation is extremely sparse at the high school level. In the Boys & Girls Clubs of America, for instance, only 10 percent of participants are ages sixteen to eighteen years. Indeed, throughout the Western world, attendance in youth

---

[2] Benson (1997); Carnegie Corporation of New York (1992); Connell, Gambone, & Smith (2000); Hawkins, Catalano, & Associates (1992); Hirsch (2005); Lerner (2004); Mahoney, Larson, & Eccles (2005); National Research Council and Institute of Medicine (2002); Noam, Biancaosa, & Dechausay (2003); Pittman, Irby, & Ferber (2000); Quinn (1999).

[3] Durlak, Weissberg & Pacchan (2010); Lauer et al. (2006); Zief, Lauver, & Maynard (2006).

[4] Gottfredson et al. (2010).

programs drops dramatically over the course of adolescence.[5] Clearly there is a need to develop more attractive after-school programs for high school youth, which made ASM, one of the country's largest programs for this group, an important program to study.

To the best of our knowledge, there is only one after-school program that focused exclusively on high school students and was evaluated via randomized design: Quantum Opportunities Program. In Quantum, youth in the intervention group were expected to receive academic activities (e.g., tutoring), development activities (e.g., problem prevention, college planning), and community service. Case management, mentoring, and a stipend were also provided. Findings from the initial evaluation and a larger, follow-up evaluation indicated a significant or marginally significant positive effect on high school graduation and greater likelihood of enrollment in some type of postsecondary schooling but no impact on test scores or problem behaviors.[6] Both evaluations reported major implementation problems, as several components were not fully implemented. In addition, almost all youth served were female.

After School Matters

ASM provides apprenticeship-type experiences to students in Chicago public high schools. ASM began in 2001 and during our research was located in sixty-five schools. In the fall of 2009, there were 305 apprenticeships across the city, which enrolled approximately 7,400 high school students per semester. An apprenticeship lasts for ten weeks in the fall and ten weeks in the spring. The apprenticeships meet for 9 hours/week (180 hours for the year). During and prior to our research, students were paid a stipend of $900/semester (equivalent to $5/hour), with adjustments for attendance.

Existing research suggested that ASM was ready for an experimental evaluation. ASM exit surveys, completed anonymously by youth over the Internet, revealed widespread youth enthusiasm for the programs. More than 80 percent of youth respondents indicated that ASM improved their ability to set a goal and work to achieve it; get things done on time; communicate clearly; and work with others on a team or group project. When asked to choose a word from a list of twenty-five possibilities that best described how they felt while in the program, the most frequently chosen descriptors were excited, comfortable, interested, and challenged, while the least

[5] Cotterell (1996).
[6] Hahn, Leavitt, & Aaron (1994); Maxfield, Schirm, & Rodriguez-Planas (2003).

frequently chosen were disrespected, unwelcome, lazy, and angry. ASM instructors also rated youth positively on varied skill domains. Although these internally generated data had not been analyzed statistically, response rates were not readily accessible, and there was no control group, the ratings provided some initial suggestion that the program is perceived positively in a variety of domains.

A number of ASM programs have been studied by qualitative researchers. Larson studied a media apprenticeship that focused on skills in using computer software and video equipment. His research revealed that students developed strong skills in teamwork as part of that experience.[7] In a separate study, Halpern observed twenty-four apprenticeships over the course of two years. He found that many youth appeared to make notable gains from program participation in the areas of discipline-specific knowledge and skill, general executive skills, social and interpersonal skills, and self-development. At the same time, he found variability in instructor quality and in program attendance (dosage). Furthermore, he noted that the typical instructor estimated that apprenticeships result in significant gains for only about 20 to 25 percent of youth.[8]

In a quasi-experimental study, ASM was associated with improved school attendance and fewer failing grades of F, and students who participated in four or more semesters of apprenticeship were 2.4 times as likely to graduate high school.[9] However, insufficient details were provided about the study methodology and the findings may reflect selection effects.

Overall, past studies of ASM suggest that it may result in positive outcomes, yet findings are inconclusive. Given the importance of ASM, we conducted a rigorous evaluation employing random assignment and assessed multiple outcome domains.

Research Questions

The evaluation reported in this appendix investigates whether assignment to and participation in ASM2009 resulted in gains in positive youth development and academic performance, as well as reductions in problem behaviors. As an organization, ASM2009 was most concerned with outcomes in the areas of positive youth development and marketable job skills. ASM2009 did not emphasize academic or problem behavior outcomes, but

[7] Larson (2007).
[8] Halpern, with Kimondo (2005).
[9] Goerge et al. (2007).

given their importance to the field, neither ASM2009 nor the investigators wanted to ignore these. We now briefly review each of these outcome domains.

Gains in Positive Youth Development
In this domain we include important values, attitudes, and skills that should change as a result of apprenticeship experiences that involve making integral contributions to successful work products or performances. These changes should be of general developmental benefit, as well as providing human and social capital that can be of specific use in the workplace. Our focus is on self-efficacy, self-regulation, occupational values, and relationships with adult authority figures and with peers.

Self-efficacy is the belief in one's own capacity to marshal the motivation, cognitive resources, and actions required to navigate challenging situations.[10] The belief in one's own ability to exercise a degree of control over life circumstances is critical because it influences "how people think, feel, motivate themselves, and act."[11] Self-efficacy influences the goals students set for themselves (e.g., students with a higher sense of self-efficacy establish increasingly challenging and difficult goals) and the commitment with which they pursue those goals.[12] Self-efficacy beliefs are impacted by four main forms of influence: (1) mastery experiences, which provide direct evidence of having what it takes to succeed at a task or challenge; (2) vicarious experiences, which provide evidence based on observation of others that the young person can succeed if others with similar characteristics can do so; (3) social persuasion experiences, which provide opportunities for youth to be convinced verbally that they are capable of success; and (4) positive physiological or emotional experiences, which generate higher self-assessments of capability than negative experiences. Educational experiences that provide these experiences should lead to self-efficacy gains, and ASM2009 apprenticeship experiences may do so as well.[13]

Self-regulation describes how individuals pursue goal-directed activities across changing situations and over time through the management of their attention and emotions.[14] Persons with high self-regulation are aware of their emotions and able to control the duration and intensity of the attentive distractions they produce, whereas individuals with low self-regulation

[10] Wood & Bandura (1989).
[11] Bandura (1995), p. 2.
[12] Zimmerman (1990, 1995b).
[13] For the last two sentences, see Bandura (1995, 1997), although he does not refer to ASM.
[14] Karoly (1993); Zimmerman (1995a).

may have difficulty disengaging sufficiently from their current emotional state to direct their attention to the task at hand.[15] Self-regulation is an important part of how students handle their own learning processes when they experience distractions from their work.[16] In addition, self-regulation is an important part of adolescents' involvement in work and career activities.[17] Self-regulation is quite salient to youth from neighborhoods that have high rates of poverty and crime, which can be quite stressful.[18]

Occupational values are the beliefs and attitudes that individuals develop toward work that influence vocational striving and work choices in life.[19] Occupational values have both intrinsic dimensions (e.g., autonomy, compatibility with one's interests and abilities) and extrinsic dimensions (e.g., money, social status). The quality of a work experience can have an impact on the formation of values about work. For example, findings from a multiwave longitudinal study of youth and occupational values by sociologist Jeylan Mortimer showed that the chance to learn useful skills on the job had a strong positive influence on the development of occupational values, which, in turn, predicted subsequent job experience. Students with stronger values were more likely to report better job experiences, suggesting both that their own orientation to work may help youth find better jobs and that they engage with the job in a manner more likely to produce a satisfactory experience. Mortimer also found that young adults whose high school jobs provided opportunities for learning new skills were much more likely to be employed seven years later in jobs they considered career related. Mortimer et al. concluded that the quality of adolescents' work experience – especially the opportunity to learn new skills and manage challenges – is the critical factor in how youth employment will ultimately impact occupational values. ASM2009 apprenticeship experiences involve learning challenging new skills and therefore may lead to increases in occupational values.

With respect to *relationships with adult authority figures*, one of the most critical challenges that young people face as they enter the workforce is to develop a satisfactory relationship with their supervisor (the "boss"). Drawing on the concept of internal working models of relationships from attachment theory,[20] it is possible that the relationship that youth develop with their ASM2009 instructors can provide them with a positive working

---

[15] Luszczynska (2004).

[16] Corno (1993); Karoly (1993).

[17] Owens & Schneider (2005).

[18] See our earlier book on Boys & Girls Clubs (Hirsch, Deutsch, & DuBois, 2011).

[19] For this paragraph, see Mortimer et al. (1996); Mortimer (2003).

[20] For example, Bretherton & Munholland (1999).

model of the kind of relationship that they can expect with their eventual workplace supervisor. Although relationships with ASM2009 instructors would not have the kind of affective, familial-like quality that occurs among early adolescents at good after-school programs,[21] prior research has shown they do mimic and anticipate the kinds of relationships that youth will encounter in the workplace.[22] Effective relationships with ASM2009 instructors should provide apprentices with a more positive orientation toward the kind of relationship they can eventually establish at work, so that they consider the supervisor as a potential mentor.[23]

In addition to forming relationships with adults, teens in ASM2009 programs are required to collaborate with other students in accomplishing apprenticeship-related goals. Experience working with other youth provides students with opportunities to *learn skills related to social development* and is a critical component of adolescent developmental processes.[24] Whether ASM2009 provided more opportunities to develop interpersonal social skills will be considered in the present investigation.

Academics

Regarding *academic performance*, The National Research Council (NRC) found that in urban high schools approximately only half of students who enter go on to receive a high school degree.[25] In this context, the most important educational outcome would appear to be student retention and, ultimately, high school graduation. Progress toward this goal would be marked by improved attendance and grades.[26] As a hard measure of academic performance, we will test whether apprentices demonstrate increased attendance and better grades.

The NRC identified a number of factors that are likely to have positive effects on urban high school students: challenging instruction and support for high standards; choices that make the curriculum relevant to adolescent long-term goals; and promoting a sense of belonging by creating a supportive social context. These factors map well onto the experiences that ASM2009 apprenticeships purported to offer youth in their high schools. Specifically, students who participate should report greater *attachment to*

---

[21] Hirsch (2005); Hirsch, Deutsch, & DuBois (2011).
[22] Halpern (2006).
[23] For the value of mentoring relationships to youth, see DuBois & Karcher (2012); Hamilton & Hamilton (2004); Rhodes (2002).
[24] Hansen, Larson, & Dworkin (2003).
[25] National Research Council and Institute of Medicine (2003).
[26] Rumberger & Larson (1998).

school through both a sense of belonging as well as a greater perception of the instrumental value of education.

Problem Behavior

A different report by the NRC, led by psychologist Jacquelynne Eccles, concluded that community youth programs decreased rates of *problem behavior*.[27] There was some question as to whether after-school programs in particular had such an effect.[28] However, a recent meta-analysis by psychologist Joseph Durlak and colleagues did find a positive effect for after-school programs on problem behavior for the more focused programs.[29] Moreover, the NRC report identifies features of positive youth settings that likely account for positive outcomes and ASM2009 would appear to load highly on most of those features. Thus participation in ASM2009 should result in reductions in rates of problem behavior.

METHOD

Characteristics of the Entire Sample

Characteristics of the recruitment process, school, and so forth, are reported in Chapter 1 and in greater detail in our Technical Report.[30] We overview this information here, as well as provide some detail not reported in Chapter 1.

Participants were Chicago public high school students. They were primarily 9th and tenth graders and were an average of 15.9 years old at the pretest survey. The majority was African American (77 percent) and low income (92 percent received free or reduced price lunch). Final analyses were limited to students with outcome measures in at least one domain (i.e., participated in the posttest assessment or we were able to obtain a school transcript). This resulted in a total of 535 students.

The majority of participants had also been involved in an extracurricular activity in the year before the study (82 percent). Students who had been in the same apprenticeship in the prior year were not allowed to be a part of the study. However, students who had been part of a different ASM2009 program (either a club or another apprenticeship program) were allowed to

---

[27] National Research Council and Institute of Medicine (2002).

[28] Gottfredson et al. (2004).

[29] Durlak & Weissberg (2010).

[30] Hirsch et al. (2011).

participate and 21 percent had prior ASM experience. Finally, 75 percent of students reported having had a prior part-time job (e.g., babysitting, yard work, fast food restaurants, grocery/convenience stores, etc.).

As noted in Chapter 1, the control group could pursue any other after-school program or activity as they normally would ("business as usual"), with the exception that they could not enter another ASM apprenticeship. The overwhelming majority of the control group (91 percent) reported involvement either in an organized after-school activity (primarily) or paid work. Thus, we were effectively comparing ASM to an alternative treatment. It is much harder to demonstrate impact when there is an alternative treatment rather than no-treatment as the comparison.

Treatment Group Determination

Intent-to-Treat Group

First, we completed analyses examining the effect of treatment assignment using the entire participant sample. Treatment was defined as having been assigned to the apprenticeship. In addition to including all those who completed treatment, it included those who dropped out (received no or a low dose of the intervention), four of whom subsequently enrolled in an alternative ASM2009 apprenticeship despite our efforts to prevent that from happening. In addition, we included in the control group for these analyses twenty-four youth who again, despite our best efforts, managed to enroll in an ASM2009 apprenticeship.

Although defining the treatment and control groups in this way may seem counterintuitive to some in the practice community, evaluation researchers privilege findings from intent-to-treat analyses. This is because dropouts from the treatment or control group threaten the randomization design. In particular, there is the worry that those who remain in treatment would be most likely to make gains under any circumstance, while those who drop out might be unlikely to improve (a form of selection effect). In addition, an important policy question is whether the treatment is effective for the entire group targeted to receive it, as public resources are spent on the entire group, not just those who remain in treatment or attend frequently.

Treatment-on-the-Treated

Many apprentices did not receive a full dose of the treatment. In fact, 47 percent of students assigned to treatment dropped out before the end of the apprenticeship. The high dropout rate is not unusual in after-school programs.[31]

ASM2009 payment guidelines state that apprentices cannot miss more than four sessions per pay period (fifteen sessions, roughly 73 percent attendance) to receive a stipend. Using this guideline, students who attended at least 73 percent of the sessions were considered to have received the intervention and were included in the treatment-on-the-treated group. Participants assigned to treatment who did not meet this attendance standard were excluded from these analyses. Demographics for the treatment-on-the-treated sample indicate that youth were an average age of 15.9 years, 79 percent were African American, 59 percent were female, and 93 percent received free or reduced price lunches. We note that these analyses excluded four treatment dropouts who enrolled in an alternative ASM2009 apprenticeship, as well as twenty-four control youth who enrolled in an alternative ASM2009 apprenticeship.

We compared those who met the ASM2009 standard for treatment dosage with those who were assigned to treatment but dropped out. Youth in the treatment-on-the-treated group were more likely to be African American (83 percent vs. 71 percent of dropouts; $p < .05$), whereas those who dropped out were more likely to be Latino/a (17 percent of treatment-on-the-treated vs. 28% of dropouts; $p < .05$). Those in the treatment-on-the-treated group were also marginally more likely to receive free or reduced priced lunch compared with those who dropped out ($p < .10$). On measures collected at the pretest survey, youth in the treatment-on-the-treated group rated themselves as having significantly higher self-efficacy ($p < .05$) and marginally higher self-regulation ($p = .10$) compared to those who dropped out. However, the pretest difference between treated youth and control group youth only approached significance on self-efficacy ($p = .093$), and did not approach significance on the other pretest, positive youth development variables.

DATA COLLECTION/RESEARCH PROCEDURES

Data Sources

Variables were assessed via multiple sources and methods: surveys of youth, archival school records, and observations by the research team.

---

[31] Gottfredson et al. (2010). We discuss in our Technical Report (Hirsch et al., 2011) how many youth dropped out of ASM2009 at each stage of the program.

Time of Assessments

All measures of positive youth development were obtained via a Web-based computer survey that was given as part of the application process prior to selection into the intervention or control groups (pretest) and at the end of the spring semester, when the apprenticeship ended (posttest). Grades and other school records were obtained from the school. Self-report problem behavior measures were obtained as part of the computer survey at pretest and posttest.

We took several steps to make sure that youth completed assessments. The pretest assessment was a part of the required application procedure for the apprenticeship. For the posttest assessment in the spring, repeated PA announcements were made at school to alert students, notification was sent to students in their homeroom at school, two phone calls were made and a letter mailed to their residence, and computer labs were reserved for our exclusive use. The computer survey and the Northwestern Mock Job Interview were scheduled together on a Saturday at their school and $50 was provided immediately on completion. Youth assigned to treatment (89%) were more likely to complete the posttest survey than those assigned to the control group (83%; $\chi^2 = 4.50, p = .03$).

Measures

Background and Control Variables
We controlled for a host of variables in our analyses. Standard demographic information was obtained from youth report (computer survey), including gender, race/ethnicity, age, grade in school, receipt of free/reduced price lunch, and mother's educational attainment (the latter two were combined in a single composite measure of socioeconomic status).[32] Youth also reported the amount of time they spent in each of five extracurricular activities, described their paid employment experiences, and reported whether they had been in an ASM apprenticeship during the prior year. From archival data, we obtained the two most recent standardized achievement test scores (for most youth, their seventh and eighth grade scores). We created a mean of reading and math stanine scores across both years and used the mean combined score as a control measure of academic ability. There were no differences between the ASM2009 group and the control group

---

[32] Adapted from Ensminer et al. (2000).

on any of these variables in both the intent-to-treat and the treatment-on-the-treated analyses.

Implementation/Process Variables
Members of the research team observed each apprenticeship weekly and wrote detailed field notes. Approximately 2,400 pages of field notes were obtained.

Dependent/Outcome Variables
We made minor modifications to many of the instruments. Specifically, some instrument response choices were rescaled and questions were reworded to make them more understandable for high school students. For some measures, we combined instruments and eliminated items to address our substantive interest and limit the length of the survey. We conducted extensive piloting to make sure the Web-based computer survey was understandable. The psychometric properties of the final instruments met accepted standards.

Positive Youth Development

Self-efficacy. We acknowledge that there is a debate whether self-efficacy is task specific. We use a measure of global self-efficacy for several reasons. First, the field is interested in whether after-school provides experiences that increase participants' global self-efficacy, which would be tapped in multiple settings and not limited to the apprenticeship experience. We were repeatedly told that ASM2009 at its best was able to "turn lives around," which suggests a global rather than highly circumscribed impact. Certainly, most of the rhetoric about the benefits of after-school, and frequently cited qualitative studies, refer to a broad rather than narrow impact.[33] Practically, to have task-specific measures of self-efficacy, we would need to assess efficacy related not only to each of the thirteen different apprenticeships, but also each of the myriad extracurricular activities engaged in by the control group. It was not realistic to have available and get good data from such a multitude of instruments, which would also need to be equivalent and each psychometrically sound.

We used Sherer's Self Efficacy Scale.[34] Sherer's scale taps a number of relevant domains, including behavior initiation, effort, and persistence. Our

[33] For example, McLaughlin, Irby, & Langman (1994).
[34] Sherer et al. (1982).

scale was comprised of 13 items that included: "When I set goals for myself, I rarely achieve them," "When I have something unpleasant to do, I stick to it until I finish it," and "I feel insecure about my ability to do things." Youth were asked to rate how much they agreed or disagreed with each of the statements. The scale had an internal reliability of α = .87.

Self-regulation. The scale taps the extent to which students are able to manage their attention and emotions as they pursue goal-directed activities. The original ten-item scale was in German and the scale authors developed an English translation[35]; we concluded that additional language modifications were necessary for suitability to the US urban high school setting. Students were asked to rate the degree they agreed or disagreed with statements such as, "I can concentrate on one activity for a long time if necessary;" "I can control my thoughts so they don't distract me from what I'm doing;" and "After an interruption, I am able to concentrate again right away." The final scale had an internal reliability of α = .83.

Occupational values. The measure is the occupational values scale from the University of Minnesota's Youth Development Study.[36] The twelve-item scale measures how important both intrinsic and extrinsic considerations are expected to be when an adolescent contemplates job seeking in his or her future. Items included "Good pay;" "Time off when I need it;" "A job that uses my skills and abilities;" and "A chance to be helpful to others or useful to society." The total scale's reliability was α = .83.

Relationships with adult authority figures. Drawing on a five-item version used in after-school research, this ten-item scale taps youth trust and caring in relation to adults and a belief that adults care about you as an individual and are interested in mentoring.[37] Items include "Adults are interested in helping you learn to be successful" and "Adults are just interested in their job, not in you." The internal reliability of the scale was α = .90.

Interpersonal relationships. We also obtained self-report on skills that youth may have learned in ASM2009 (or in their most time-intensive extracurricular activity for control youth) about how to work with others. We created an instrument using items from Youth Experience Survey,[38] supplemented with items from Mortimer's Youth Development Survey. Items included "I learned to work with others on a team or group project;" "I learned how my emotions and attitude affect others;" and "I learned to be

---

[35] Luszczunska et al. (2004).
[36] Mortimer (2003).
[37] Hirsch, Deutsch, & DuBois (2011).
[38] Hansen & Larson (2002).

able to give feedback." Factor analysis confirmed measurement of a single construct tapping peer social skills; the final measure had a high internal reliability of α = .94.

Academic Outcomes

School performance. We obtained information on grades and attendance from school records. Grade point average (GPA) was calculated using weighted grades from students' core academic courses. We also used the number of failed core courses as an outcome measure.

School attendance. We used the number of days students were absent for each semester (and the total year) as reported on student transcripts.

Attitudes about school. Attitudes about school are measured using the Identification with School Questionnaire.[39] The total scale included fifteen items tapping students' self-reports of (1) a feeling of belonging at school and (2) a belief that school contributes to one's future success. Items include "I feel that I am treated with respect at school;" "I'd rather be anywhere else than in school;" and "Most of what I learn in school will be useful when I get a job." The two subscales (Belonging and Extrinsic Value, respectively) were validated in confirmatory factor analysis[40] and had acceptable internal reliability in our sample (Whole scale α = .78; Belonging α = .73; Extrinsic value α = .63).

Problem Behaviors

A ten-item youth self-report measure of problem behaviors was taken from the National Longitudinal Study of Adolescent Health (Add Health).[41] The scale includes measures from Add Health In-Home Interview from Wave II: Section 23 on Contraception; Section 27 on Tobacco, Alcohol, & Drugs; Section 28 on Delinquency; and Section 29 on Fighting and Violence. A total score was computed which represents the mean score across all ten items (α = .77).

Data Analysis Overview
Readers who do not have a background in advanced statistics may choose to skim over or skip this section.

---

[39] Voelkl (1996).
[40] Voelkl (1996).
[41] Undry (1998).

We analyzed the data using a hierarchical linear model (HLM) approach.[42] We carried out an HLM analysis for each of the continuous dependent variables separately. A two-level hierarchical linear model was estimated where the level 1 model is a within-apprenticeship-choice model. The level 2 model is an across apprenticeship model that could include apprenticeship-specific treatment effects. Because the students who select the same apprenticeship are likely to be more similar than those who select different apprenticeships, the sample is clustered by apprenticeship choice. In experimental design terminology, the apprenticeship choices are blocks and individual students are the replications within blocks. Because individuals within blocks are randomly assigned to treatments, the design is a (generalized) randomized blocks design with apprenticeships crossed with treatments.[43] Because the purpose of this study is to evaluate the effects of the apprenticeships that are part of the study and not to generalize to a broader population of apprenticeships, we treat the apprenticeships as having fixed effects in our analysis.

The specific level 1 model for the continuous outcomes can be described as follows. Let Y_{ij} be the outcome score of the *j*th student who selected the *i*th apprenticeship

$$Y_{ij} = \beta_{oi} + \beta_{1i}PRETEST_{ij} + \beta_{2i}MALE_{ij} + \beta_{3i}BLACK_{ij} + \beta_{4i}SES_{ij} + \beta_{5i}AGE_{ij} + \beta_{6i}WORKEXP_{ij} + \beta_{7i}EXTRACURRIC_{ij} + \beta_{8i}PRIOR_{ij} + \beta_{9i}TREATMENT_{ij} + e_{ij}$$

where $PRETEST_{ij}$ is a covariate matched to the outcome, $MALE_{ij}$ is a dummy variable for gender, $BLACK_{ij}$ is a dummy variable for African American, SES_{ij} is a composite socioeconomic status variable (created from self-report free/reduced price lunch qualification and mother's educational attainment), AGE_{ij} is a measure of student age in years and months, $WORKEXP_{ij}$ is a dummy for work experience as reported at the pretest survey, $EXTRACURRIC_{ij}$ is a mean score of the amount of time spent across five extracurricular activities as reported at the pretest survey, $PRIOR_{ij}$ is a dummy variable for prior participation in an ASM program, $TREATMENT_{ij}$ is a dummy variable for the treatment condition, and e_{ij} is a student-specific residual. In this model, β_{1i}, β_{2i}, β_{3i}, β_{4i}, β_{5i}, β_{6i}, β_{7i}, β_{8i} and β_{9i} are the effects of *PRETEST, MALE, BLACK, SES, AGE, WORKEXP, EXTRACURRIC, PRIOR,* and *TREATMENT* in apprenticeship *i*.

---

[42] Raudenbush & Bryk (2002).
[43] Kirk (1995).

For most of the outcome variables examined in this appendix, the covariate we have labeled *PRETEST* is the same variable as the outcome, measured prior to the beginning of the intervention. The exception is academic outcomes. For academic performance, we controlled for prior academic ability, as measured by a composite measure averaging the two most recent reading and math standardized test stanine scores.

We treat apprenticeship selection as a fixed effect, so the specific level 2 model for the level 1 intercept is

$$\beta_{oi} = \pi_{oo} + \eta_{oi},$$

where π_{oo} is the control group average across apprenticeships and η_{oj} is an apprenticeship-specific residual. The level 2 model for the other covariates is

$$\beta_{1i} = \pi_{10},$$
$$\beta_{2i} = \pi_{20},$$
$$\beta_{3i} = \pi_{30},$$
$$\beta_{4i} = \pi_{40},$$
$$\beta_{5i} = \pi_{50},$$
$$\beta_{6i} = \pi_{60},$$
$$\beta_{7i} = \pi_{70},$$
$$\beta_{8i} = \pi_{80},$$

so that the effects of the covariates are constrained to be equal across groups. In the primary analysis, the level 2 model for the treatment effect is

$$\beta_{9i} = \pi_{90}$$

so that we will be estimating and testing the average treatment effect across apprenticeships (π_{90}) controlling for the covariates.

The main object of the primary analysis for each dependent variable is to estimate and test the statistical significance of the average apprenticeship effect π_{90}.

RESULTS

Implementation

Our observations and qualitative interviews did not reveal any major implementation problems aside from the high attrition rate. Consistent with the quantitative data from the program design measure reported in

Chapter 1, all programs were operated according to the ASM2009 model; in particular, there was a strong emphasis on developing skills in all of the apprenticeships. There were no instances when programs did not meet for extended periods or did not obtain needed equipment within a reasonable time period. In two programs, a co-instructor was absent for significant stretches in the second semester for personal reasons. We should note, however, that there was more variation in the quality of implementation across apprenticeships than we had anticipated, given that we preselected for the better apprenticeships. Chapter 3 compares apprenticeships that vary in the quality of implementation.

Impact Findings: Intent-to-Treat

We first completed analyses examining the effect of treatment assignment using the entire participant sample. For this set of analyses, the treatment group was defined as having been assigned to the apprenticeship (which included those who received treatment and those who dropped out). As noted, the great majority of control group youth were involved in an alternative activity.

Positive Youth Development Outcomes

There was a significant treatment effect for one of the five outcomes in this domain: self-regulation. Both the treatment ($M = 3.99$, $SD = .59$ at T1; $M = 3.88$, $SD = .62$ at Time 2) and control group ($M = 4.01$, $SD = .54$ at T1; $M = 3.79$, $SD = .62$ at T2) declined in self-reported ratings of self-regulation from pre- to posttest; however, treatment group means declined significantly less than the control group ($t = 2.14$, $g = .18$, $p = .033$), indicating a preventive impact. Results for the four other outcomes in this domain – self-efficacy, adult relationships, occupational values, and interpersonal learning – were not significant.

Academic Outcomes

Academic performance outcomes were assessed using weighted grade point average and number of core courses failed for each semester. For these analyses, students' standardized test scores were used as a pretest control. In terms of weighted GPA for the study year, there was no difference between ASM2009 youth and control youth. Neither was there a difference for number of failed courses. We also examined GPA and number of failed courses by semester and once again there were no significant findings.

Because prior year attendance was not available for many of the students in the study, we estimated two separate HLM models for impact of ASM2009 on attendance: one using the subsample of participants with available prior year attendance records and a second for the entire sample. We were able to obtain prior year attendance only for students who attended the same school the prior year (i.e., nontransfer students in grades 10–12 during the evaluation year). The results indicate that there were no significant treatment effects for school attendance. For the larger sample of all students, we tested for treatment effects using a model with standardized test scores as an additional covariate, hypothesizing that students who have higher academic ability may be more likely to attend school. There were no significant differences in these analyses, either.

Students' perception of school was assessed at posttest only. Given that students with greater academic ability may be more likely to see value in school and to feel welcome, we estimated a model controlling for standardized test scores. Treatment youth had a marginally higher mean score ($M = 4.05$, $SD = .46$) for the overall Identification with School Questionnaire compared to the control group ($M = 3.94$, $SD = .50$, $t = 2.22$, $g = .23$, $p = .059$). The difference with respect to extrinsic value also favored treatment youth but was also only marginally significant ($p = .07$). There was no significant or marginally significant difference in sense of belonging.

Problem Behaviors

HLM analyses estimated impacts controlling for background variables and the pretest measure. There was a significant overall scale difference favoring treatment youth. Both groups reported a slight rise in problem behavior, but the rise was less for those assigned to ASM2009 ($M = 1.13$, $SD = .22$ to $M = 1.20$, $SD = .30$) than for control youth ($M = 1.16$, $SD = .28$ to $M = 1.28$, $SD = .53$; $t = -1.95$, $g = -.12$, $p = .05$), suggesting a preventive impact. Because of the policy interest in these variables, we also examined scores on the individual items. These suggest that the scale difference was driven by the crime items. Youth assigned to ASM2009 ($M = 1.03$, $SD = .28$ to $M = 1.03$, $SD = .21$) were significantly less likely to report increased sale of drugs at post than were control youth ($M = 1.07$, $SD = .49$ to $M = 1.16$, $SD = .70$; $t = -2.61$, $g = -.19$, $p = .01$); ASM2009 youth ($M = 1.05$, $SD = .34$ to $M = 1.07$, $SD = .39$) also reported significantly less increase in gang activity over time than control youth ($M = 1.07$, $SD = .42$ to $M = 1.18$, $SD = .78$; $t = -2.01$, $g = -.15$, $p < .05$). There was a marginal effect ($p < .07$) favoring ASM2009 for stealing items worth more than $50.

We next considered whether treatment differences in these problem behaviors might be related to involvement in extracurricular activities (including paid employment). More time spent in extracurricular activities, for example, leaves less time to be engaged in criminal activity during the 3–6 PM peak period. Although 91 percent of control youth participated in some structured after-school activity, it also was the case that 87 percent of ASM2009 youth participated in an activity in addition to ASM2009. There were no significant between-group differences in extracurricular participation rates.

It does not appear that the control group youth spent as much time overall in their activities as ASM2009 youth spent in the combination of their ASM2009 apprenticeship and other activities. When we looked at time investment across five types of non-ASM2009 activities – sports, music/performance, service, community, and academic – it was only in sports that the control group spent significantly more time than did ASM2009 youth (Kruskal–Wallis $\chi^2 = 6.55$, $p = .01$). However, even here the difference between control youth (26 percent) and ASM2009 youth (20 percent) who participated more than once per week (the most intensive involvement on our scale) was not substantial. When one adds together time ASM2009 youth spent in ASM2009 (three times per week) and outside of ASM2009, it appears likely that they spent more time in structured after-school activities than did the control group, though our measures do not allow us to test this directly.

Youth income may also impact involvement in these particular problem behaviors. In terms of paid employment outside of ASM2009, control youth were significantly more likely to report a paid job (23 percent) than ASM2009 youth (14 percent; $\chi^2 = 5.37$, $p < .03$). However, there were no significant differences between the groups (for non-ASM2009 positions) in terms of hourly wages, hours worked per week, or weekly earnings. Thus, if one adds in the additional $45/week stipend that many ASM2009 youth received for their apprenticeships, it seems likely that ASM2009 youth received more earnings than did control youth, and thus may have less need to engage in remunerative illegal activities, although we do not have definitive data about this.

A detailed power analysis and examination of heterogeneity of treatment effects may be found in our Technical Report.

Treatment-on-the-Treated Findings

In this section, we report findings for those who *received* treatment using ASM2009's attendance standard. Again, we note that 47 percent of students assigned to treatment dropped out before the end of the apprenticeship.

As with the intent-to-treat analyses, we ran HLM analyses for all dependent variable measures separately. Each model included key demographic variables and, when available, a matched pretest measure covariate. Again, we defined treatment participation using ASM2009's own standard for treatment dosage, which was a 73 percent attendance rate. The following reports findings in each of the key outcome domains using this treatment definition.

Positive Youth Development Outcomes

The only significant treatment effect was for self-regulation ($p = .03$). Self-regulation means declined for both treatment and control groups, but declined significantly less for the treatment group. These findings parallel those in the intent-to-treat analysis. The difference in relative decline translates to a positive treatment effect of $g = .19$ of a standard deviation after controlling for the pretest measure.

Treatment effects for the other four positive youth development outcomes failed to reach significance.

Academic Outcomes

Academic performance. Academic performance outcomes were assessed using weighted GPA and number of core courses failed for each semester. For these analyses, student standardized test scores were used as a pretest control. Analyses revealed that there were no significant treatment effects for grade point average or for number of courses failed.

With respect to attendance effects, prior year attendance was available for only some of the students in the study. There were no significant treatment effects in analyses that controlled for prior year's attendance.

We also completed a second analysis using the entire sample of students. In this analysis, standardized test scores were used as an additional covariate. Overall, students in the apprenticeship were absent fewer days in the fall semester ($M = 9.42$, $SD = 7.26$) compared with the control group ($M = 11.37$, $SD = 10.12$). This difference translates into a treatment effect of $g = -.22$. The treatment effect was significant for the fall semester (t-ratio $= -2.02$, $p = .04$), There was no significant difference between the apprenticeship and control groups for spring attendance, and the treatment effect for the whole year was marginal (t-ratio $= -1.68$, $p = .09$).

Attitudes about school. Because there was no pretest assessment, we ran a model controlling for student standardized test scores. Overall, apprentices

(M = 4.08, SD = .47) had a higher identification with school compared to the control group (M = 3.94, SD = .51, t-ratio = 2.3, p = .023). Apprentices (M = 4.27, SD = .54) saw increased value in school compared to control group students (M = 4.09, SD = .55, t-ratio = 2.74, p < .01), yielding a treatment effect size of g = .33. There were no significant differences between the groups on the belonging subscale.

Problem Behaviors

There was no significant difference between the treatment and control groups on the composite index. We should note that as in the intent-to-treat analyses, apprentices reported selling drugs significantly less than controls in the treatment-on-the-treated analyses; however, this result needs to be viewed with caution given the lack of an overall scale effect in the treatment-on-the-treated analysis. There was no significant difference regarding participation in gang activity.

DISCUSSION

After School Matters is one of the largest and best known after-school programs for high school students in the country. It is based on an apprenticeship-like model that involves young people in paid, project-based learning experiences in a wide array of fields, from the arts to technology. Prior studies suggested that ASM2009 could lead to important gains, laying the foundation for this study.

This evaluation research had a number of strengths: it utilized a randomized controlled trial, which provides the best way to separate program effects from selection effects; multiple outcomes were assessed across four domains, permitting a comprehensive look at possible effects; data were obtained via multiple methods from a variety of sources, minimizing the potential bias inherent in any one type of data; extensive process data were obtained to provide a better understanding of underlying processes; and statistical techniques were employed so that we could correct for clustered sampling. The selection of experienced ASM2009 instructors was designed to enable us to test whether ASM2009 works when, on balance, it is implemented well.

In what follows, we first synthesize the outcome results to consider the effectiveness of these ASM2009 apprenticeships compared to the experiences of youth in the control group, most of whom were involved in alternative activities. Are there benefits to ASM2009 above and beyond those obtained from participation in alternative activities? We will present both positive and skeptical responses that can reasonably be made to this query. We then offer our own conclusions and turn toward the future, considering future directions for ASM2009 as a program and for evaluation research on after-school programs.

Comparative Effectiveness of ASM2009 Apprenticeships

We first consider the results in terms of specific outcomes, and then turn to consider results in terms of average effects per outcome domain.

Specific Outcomes: Self-Regulation, Problem Behavior, and Academics

The two scales on which significant effects were found are substantively important and their impacts can be reasonably explained by participation in ASM2009 versus control group activities. Self-regulation is an important personal skill that taps how well youth are able to pursue goal-directed activities through the management of their attention and emotions.[44] ASM2009 apprenticeships provided support for such skill development during most program sessions, particularly through their emphasis on a specific project. Project demands, underscored by deadlines, and the likelihood that the product would be viewed by outsiders, provide a structure that motivates one to maintain focus on the tasks at hand in spite of distractions.[45] The findings on the design features measure (Chapter 1) indicate that ASM2009 was more successful at providing this structure than were the alternative activities in which control youth participated.

The finding that ASM2009 youth reported less of an increase in problem behavior over time, particularly in relation to criminal acts such as selling drugs and participation in gang activities, is the result that is most likely to resonate in the policy world. There are several possible explanations for this finding. First, even when accounting for participation in non-ASM2009 extracurricular activities, it appears that ASM2009 youth spent more time in structured, after-school activities than did control youth. The after-school hours, particularly 3–6 PM, are well known as the period when youth are most at risk to be the victims or perpetrators of crime.[46] Thus, ASM2009 youth are more likely to be unavailable during the highest risk period to

---

[44] Gestsdottir & Lerner (2008); Karol (1993); Luszczynska, et al. (2004); Owens & Schneider (2005); Zimmerman (1995a,b).

[45] In intensive qualitative research at Boys & Girls Clubs, we found that conditions at the site helped distract youth from what could often be overwhelming stress in their lives (Hirsch, Deutsch, & DuBois, 2011, especially chapter 3 on "Pocahontas").

[46] Snyder & Sickmund (1999).

engage in juvenile crime. Second, when combining their ASM2009 stipend with non-ASM2009 work wages, it appears that ASM2009 youth had higher earnings than did control youth. Accordingly, they may have less need for the financial benefits that can accrue from selling drugs or participating in gang actions. Finally, ASM2009 design features may have led apprentices to be more likely to believe that there was a place for them in the adult employment world, an important developmental concern for adolescents.[47] This may have ledASM2009 apprentices to have more positive expectations of meaningful adult employment and consequently less likely to jeopardize their perceived future for the short-term benefit of criminal activity.

Given that ASM2009 did not provide academic instruction, it is not surprising that there was no impact on school grades. A prior, quasi-experimental study of ASM had found such an effect,[48] but it is likely that this represented selection effects. The Quantum Opportunities evaluation found some significant effects on academic outcomes, but Quantum had program components that specifically targeted academic skills.[49] We also found no evidence of improved school attendance due to ASM2009 participation and only a trend for ASM2009 youth to have more positive attitudes toward school. Improvement in the latter domain could ultimately impact attendance, which in turn could impact academic performance. Furthermore, it is possible that a greater emphasis in ASM on teaching marketable job skills, which could increase the perceived external value of school, could lead to positive changes in these areas.

Averaging Effects within Outcome Domain
It is not unusual for treatment effects to be averaged within a particular outcome domain in meta-analyses or in reports such as those conducted by the What Works Clearinghouse. Such averages reflect treatment effects on broader constructs than any single measure. As ASM2009 posited effects in broad outcome domains, this approach is appropriate for this evaluation. Given the large number of nonsignificant effects, it is not surprising that the average treatment effects within domains are small (see Table A1.1). We include the findings from the mock job interview in that table to help provide a more comprehensive view of ASM2009.

How do these results compare to other evaluations of after-school programs in the literature? Are the ASM2009 effects stronger or weaker than

---

[47] Erikson (1968).
[48] Goerge et al. (2007).
[49] Hahn et al. (1994); Maxfield et al. (2003).

TABLE A1.1 *Average effect size by outcome domain*

Domain	ASM ITT[a]	ASM TOT[b]	Durlak et al. (2010) meta-analysis		
			All 68 programs	SAFE	Non-SAFE
Positive Youth Development (Self-Perceptions)	.03	.03	.34	.37	.13
Marketable Job Skills	−.02	.08	–	–	–
Academics	–	–	–	–	–
Grades	−.02	.12	.12	.22	.05
Attendance	.09	.05	.10	.14	.07
School Identification (Bonding)	.20	.25	.14	.25	.03
Problem Behavior	.09	.11	.19	.30	.08

[a] Average effect sizes calculated using the intent-to-treat analysis.
[b] Average effect sizes calculated using the treatment-on-the-treated analysis.

has typically been found? We shall compare the ASM2009 findings to those reported in two meta-analyses, each of which has its strengths and limitations.[50]

Durlak et al.'s 2010 meta-analysis of after-school programs that seek to promote personal and social skills provides the most comprehensive comparative data. Across all sixty-eight studies in the review, there was an overall mean effect size of 0.22, which involved averaging all effects within a single study and then averaging across studies. Their outcome domains do not correspond exactly with those of this evaluation; their domain of child self-perceptions is most similar to our positive youth development, and they do not report an overall academic domain, instead presenting effects for school grades, school attendance, and school bonding (which in our study is the measure of school identification). In looking at Table A1.1, we can see that the ASM2009 effects for positive youth development (child self-perceptions), school attendance, and problem behavior are less; the ASM2009 effects are roughly equivalent for grades, but higher for school identification (bonding).

Durlak et al. go on to classify the after-school programs in their review in terms of whether they are SAFE (i.e., sequenced, active, focused, and

[50] We will use the ASM2009 treatment-on-the-treated figures as these map more closely unto those reported in the Durlak et al. meta-analysis.

explicit). Significant effects were found only for those programs that were classified as SAFE (i.e., positive ratings on all four SAFE dimensions). We asked Durlak whether ASM2009 would have been included in his review given the nature of the program and whether ASM2009 would be classified as SAFE. After reading a draft of our Technical Report, Durlak concluded that ASM2009 would have been included in his review. In terms of whether ASM2009 constituted a SAFE program, Durlak indicated that he would rate it as having sequenced and active learning strategies, but not focused and explicit interventions with respect to the outcome of socioemotional learning. Compared to SAFE programs, ASM2009 had smaller effect sizes for self-perceptions, grades, school attendance and problem behavior; the effect sizes were equal for school identification (see Table A1.1). Compared to non-SAFE programs, ASM2009 had stronger effects for school identification and grades; roughly equivalent effects for school attendance and problem behavior; and weaker effects for positive youth development.

There are several limitations of the Durlak et al. review for our purposes. Only 35 percent of the studies they reviewed involved random assignment. It is possible that the average effect sizes are overestimates, as more rigorous, experimental studies may obtain weaker effects. In addition, only 9 percent of the studies involved programs serving high school youth. Finally, many of the studies did not determine whether members of the comparison group were participating in alternative, formal after-school activities, so it is unclear whether they constitute a no-treatment or an alternative treatment control group. One would expect stronger effects if treatment was being compared to a no-treatment control.

A meta-analysis by Zief, Lauver, and Maynard focused exclusively on experimental evaluations of after-school programs.[51] The effect sizes found in these studies were, indeed, lower than those found in the Durlak et al. review. Unfortunately, only five studies were available, none of which focused on high school youth. Moreover, all of the programs they reviewed included an academic component, which ASM2009 did not have.

How do we weight all of these considerations? Most of us probably would like from this study a clear, definitive conclusion as to ASM2009's effectiveness or, more precisely, its added value compared to the experiences of the control group. However, we believe that there are two contrasting interpretations of these findings, each of which is reasonable. To best appreciate

---

[51] Zief, Lauver, and Maynard (2006).

what this study does and does not tell us, we thought it best to elaborate each of these perspectives before offering our own conclusions.

A Positive View of the Evaluation Findings

This perspective emphasizes that significant positive effects on important outcomes were found. Although the treatment-on-the-treated comparisons make the most intuitive sense in the program world, the most convincing findings to methodologists will be those from the intent-to-treat analyses. Given the considerable attrition in the ASM2009 sample, the youth who remained in the treatment group may differ from the original, randomly assigned treatment group. Indeed, we found that those who remained in the treatment group reported higher self-efficacy and marginally higher self-regulation prior to group assignment than did those youth who were originally assigned to treatment but subsequently dropped out. The treatment-on-the treated findings may thus represent selection effects (the stronger youth remained in treatment). The intent-to-treat analyses examine the ASM2009 and control groups as originally assigned and thus remove a selection effect as a rival hypothesis. So when significant findings are obtained from intent-to-treat analyses, as was the case for the self-regulation and problem behavior scales, this should be convincing to those who are hardest to convince. Indeed, the strongest findings came from the strongest methodology.

The two scales on which significant effects were found – self-regulation and problem behavior – are substantively important. The problem behavior impact in particular is likely to resonate in the policy world. Moreover, the credibility and meaningfulness of these two findings are enhanced because they can be linked to specific components of the ASM2009 experience that differed from the experience of control youth in alternative activities.

ASM2009 programs were found to have stronger design features than the extracurricular programs in which control youth participated (Chapter 1). These design features – including teaching specific skills, youth having a choice in activities, getting feedback on how to improve – have considerable support in the educational literature and in the 2002 National Research Council (2002) report on youth programs.[52] Correlational analyses supported their value, as those design variables were significantly associated

---

[52] For example, Edelson (2001); Brown & Camione (1996); Rogoff (1990); Schank (1995).

with several outcome variables in our dataset (these correlations may be found in our Technical Report).

ASM2009 was able to obtain positive results despite several factors that worked against doing so. For example, although the research design specified the selection of experienced instructors with high skills, not all of the instructors proved to be superior. In addition, several of the programs had low attendance. Both of these factors should have decreased the effectiveness of ASM2009, but significant effects were still obtained. It is possible that effects would have been less if one had selected a wider range of instructors, but that is speculation; the findings that are available indicate that there are positive effects.

Most initial randomized trials are efficacy studies in which programs receive a considerable amount of extra support, especially in ongoing consultation to improve implementation, which increases the likelihood of positive outcomes. However, very little extra support was provided to the ASM2009 apprenticeships in the study; there were efforts to get them supplies in a timely manner, a feedback session for executives and regional directors regarding instructors' lack of focus on linkage between the apprenticeships and the work world, and a one-session workshop for apprentices on job interview skills. In terms of support, these efforts are more in line with those of an effectiveness trial under typical implementation conditions, rather than the generous extra resources provided in efficacy trials. It is harder to obtain significant effects in effectiveness trials.

Almost all control group youth were involved in an alternative extracurricular activity or in paid work. This exposure meant that we needed to consider the control group as receiving an alternative treatment rather than as a no-treatment control. Clearly it is more difficult to find a treatment effect when the comparison group is also receiving treatment. Moreover, given that the comparison group had equivalent results on the social climate measures (see Chapter 3), which tap important program dimensions, it is reasonable to consider them a strong comparison group. This increased the difficulty of finding a significant ASM2009 treatment effect.

Finally, no significant negative effects were found in which control youth performed better than ASM2009 youth. Negative effects have been found for some after-school programs.[53]

---

[53] For example, James-Burdumy, Dynarski, & Deke (2008).

In summary, the positive perspective on the ASM2009 evaluation emphasizes the significant positive effects that were found despite a number of high bars to obtaining such results.

A Skeptical View of the Evaluation Findings

The skeptical perspective emphasizes that weak effects were found under conditions in which stronger effects should have been obtained. The study purposefully employed the better ASM2009 instructors, maximizing the potential for finding strong, significant effects. All of the instructors had at least one year of experience and almost all had several years of experience. By contrast, there was no effort to obtain the best instructors or group leaders among the extracurricular programs of the control group youth.

Despite these advantages, when significant findings were obtained, the effect sizes were not large. Although there are no universally agreed on standards for interpreting the strength of effect sizes, the typical view would likely be that the size of the self-regulation and problem behavior effects are not strong. When one examines the average effect size per domain across all four domains, the ASM2009 effects appear weak. Although ASM2009's most important outcome is positive youth development, the average effect size in that domain is close to zero. There are no significant effects at all for ASM2009's second most important outcome domain, marketable job skills.

In summary, this perspective emphasizes that only a few significant effects were found, effect sizes were typically small, and that testing a more representative sample of ASM2009 instructors may well eliminate the few positive impacts that were found.

Conclusions and Future Directions

We believe that each of these perspectives makes reasonable points, but that it is unwise to view this as a situation in which one needs to choose only one or the other. Although our culture increasingly expects a simple thumbs-up or thumbs-down summary judgment, it is important to take a more complex, historical perspective that considers how social science and program practice can interact over time. Very few randomized evaluation studies have been done on after-school programs and to the best of our knowledge only one such study has been done with an exclusively high school sample. High quality evaluation studies can provide information that is crucial for strengthening the ability of programs to produce strong effects. In turn, redeveloped programs need to be subjected to further evaluation, which can result in a cumulative process that greatly enhances program effectiveness. The after-school world is just at the beginning of this process.

Within this broader context, we consider the ASM2009 impacts to be promising. Although it is frequently the case that no significant treatment effects are found in experimental evaluation studies, in this research ASM2009 did have a significant impact in areas that are important to adolescent development and to policy. Moreover, it demonstrated these impacts in relation to what was essentially an alternative treatment comparison group. Nonetheless, we consider the counterarguments from the skeptical perspective to be serious and these force us to view the outcomes with some caution. The caution is with respect primarily to whether the average ASM2009 apprenticeship (which we did not study) is likely to provide outcomes superior to what high school youth can obtain in alternative extracurricular activities, after-school programs, and part-time jobs. The skeptical perspective may ultimately prove prescient with respect to what such an outcome study would reveal. To maximize the likelihood that the modal ASM2009 apprenticeship proves superior in such a future outcome evaluation, it is important to improve the program model.

What, then, are some important lessons for the future that can be learned from this study?

For Research

Researchers can help the field to progress in a number of ways. Elaborated change models are needed that are based both on theory and on accumulating empirical findings. Such models should focus not only on the outcomes, but the pathways or mechanisms through which different outcomes are achieved over time (and perhaps over a longer time frame than employed in this research). It is critical that potential effects be more clearly conceptualized and new measurement instruments developed. We did this for marketable job skills, but much work remains to be done with respect to positive youth development. Existing measures in that domain have been taken primarily from research on child and adolescent development or from child clinical studies, but there are large gaps between available instrumentation and some of the youth changes that we heard described by program staff. There is still uncertainty regarding exactly what and how outcomes should be measured within the still emerging area of positive youth development and more progress needs to be made in this area. This should not be surprising given that, by contrast, there has been much more thinking and research about youth problem behavior over many more years (indeed, decades).

We have acknowledged that there is a debate as to whether certain types of effects are domain-specific or global, which is relevant to the selection of measures. In this study, the variable most implicated in this debate was our global measure of self-efficacy. The domain specific argument is that gains in self-efficacy with respect to math, for example, do not automatically translate to self-efficacy gains in science, or to the academic domain more generally. Unfortunately, there are practical difficulties in conducting domain-specific assessment over all the domains we would have needed to assess; in this study, this would include not only the thirteen apprenticeships, but also the myriad extracurricular activities and jobs of control group youth. We have also found it necessary to conduct interviews with control youth regarding which activity they should be rating to obtain valid data.[54] Beyond technical issues in methodology, it is important to consider that documenting gains in global self-efficacy may well have more impact on policy makers than gains in a highly circumscribed activity (especially in what may be considered esoteric arts activities). Thus, the incremental cost and utility of domain-specific assessment needs to be considered and not just its theoretical rationale.

The extent of control group participation in alternative activities came as a surprise. ASM2009 had indicated to us that few such activities were available to this population of Chicago youth. Several school principals seconded this notion to us in preliminary operational meetings. The empirical research literature suggests a higher participation rate than our local estimates. National estimates for participation in at least one structured activity hover between 70 and 80 percent,[55] though there are consistent findings that low-income youth are underrepresented in organized activities.[56]

It is very difficult to find a precise published figure for the participation rate for a sample that is demographically comparable to ASM2009 youth. In the only instance that we were able to identify, Pederson and Seidman reported that between 38 and 42 percent of the urban, low-income high school youth in their study participated in an organized school-based activity and between 23 and 26 percent participated in such a non-school activity.[57] They do not report an overall participation rate across both types

---

[54] Mekinda & Hirsch (2010).

[55] Bouffard (2006); Feldman & Matjasko (2005); Mahoney et al. (2009).

[56] Bartko & Eccles (2003); Feldman & Matjasko (2005); McNeal (1998); Pedersen & Seidman (2005).

[57] Pederson & Seidman (2005).

of activity, though it clearly would be less than the participation rate for our control group (91 percent).[58] Differences in sample selection were likely a major factor accounting for our higher participation rate. In the other studies cited, researchers sampled the school population at large, which likely included many students with no structured, after-school activity involvement. In this study, all of the control youth had already sought to enroll in an after-school activity (i.e., ASM2009). We know from prior quantitative research that many young people who engage in one activity participate in others as well,[59] so the control youth were students likely to seek out additional activities when ASM2009 was not available. This would be consistent with findings from qualitative studies that depict a distinct culture of highly involved students who are well-networked, well-informed of after-school opportunities, and encouraged by friends, teachers, and activity leaders to attend.[60]

For purposes of evaluation research, to best understand program effects and their magnitude, more effort needs to be invested in documenting and understanding the experience of control groups. If treatment outcomes are determined by comparison to the experiences of controls, then the control group experience needs sufficient attention to justify interpretations that can have a profound effect on programs and policy. Both quantitative and qualitative studies of control groups are needed. These studies need to go beyond documentation of participation rates to consider as well the quality of control group experiences.

Finally, there is the issue of cost effectiveness. We did not collect data on ASM2009 operating costs or the costs associated with the activities of control group youth. The issue of cost needs to be considered together with benefits for policy purposes.

For Programs

Our quantitative and qualitative findings indicate that ASM2009 programs need strengthening. This should not be a surprise or a disappointment;

---

[58] Pederson and Seidman (2005) also reported that between 49 and 55 percent played team sports, but the phrasing of the item made it likely that youth would be counted who engaged in pickup games in a gym or playground setting that did not include adult involvement. If a substantial proportion of this group participated in an organized sports team led by an adult, then the cumulative involvement of that sample would more closely approach our figure.

[59] Feldman & Matjasko (2007).

[60] Flores-Gonzalez (2002, 2005); Quiroz, Gonzalez, & Frank (1996).

indeed, this is what evaluation research needs to find if the field is to advance.

Our observations revealed that ASM2009 youth need to be more fully engaged. Too much time was spent surfing the Web or socializing with each other. Greater effort also needs to be put into building high quality products or performances. To realize the potential of the ASM2009 design features, much more attention needs to be paid to engage youth throughout a session. These are really fundamental principles of youth programs, so we will not elaborate on them here. But that should not be taken as a reflection that they are unimportant. ASM2009 needed to spend a lot more time getting the basics down a lot better. This was true not only for instructors, but also for their supervisors, who often did not seem to know how to improve the performance of seriously deficient instructors.

Although many apprentices, in normal ASM2009 practice, remain enrolled for more than one semester, in our study many instructors had difficulty in developing experiences in the second semester that differed meaningfully from those in the first semester. Apprentices often did learn to perform skills faster and better in the second semester, but the importance of such developmental gains were not always communicated to youth by the instructors. Because of dropouts, many apprenticeships enrolled new students in the second semester (none of those new enrollees became subjects in our study). We were surprised by how quickly they came up to speed with those who had been continuously enrolled; had new, more advanced skills been taught, presumably this would have happened less quickly, if at all. In our view, instructors need much more training and supervision in how to develop additional, sequenced experiences over time, in how to build, in effect, a curriculum that deepens over more than one semester.

ASM2009 can learn some important implementation lessons from its own best practices. Chapter 4 discusses what lessons may be learned from an examination of two of the best apprenticeships in our evaluation.

ASM2009 needs to focus more on transferable skills. This was especially evident regarding marketable job skills, which ASM2009 has always highlighted as one of its primary concerns. Given that many of these apprenticeships focused on occupations in which the number of jobs were quite limited (especially true for arts apprenticeships), the broader utility of the skills for different occupations needs to be considered. The human resource interviewers indicated that this is always a major focus in interviewing for entry-level jobs.

Similar efforts at transferring knowledge, attitudes, and skills could be made regarding positive youth development. This would draw on the domain-specific argument in the measurement debate alluded to earlier as an impetus for innovative program development. Youth who learn skills in self-regulation in ASM2009, for example, could be explicitly trained to apply those in other situations. They could learn how to apply a new sense of self-efficacy gained in a specific after-school activity to other activities both in and out of school. This new direction would be consistent with findings regarding SAFE interventions from the Durlak et al. after-school meta-analysis: the program should be focused on and clearly emphasize specific skills.[61] It was clearly the SAFE programs that produced the best results. A promising – and critical – new direction for the future is to focus explicitly on transferable skills.

In terms of implementation, there are important questions regarding how well apprenticeship instructors, trained in a specific craft, would be interested and skilled in providing such transfer-focused instruction. It may be necessary for ASM2009, and similar programs, to provide in-house consultants who work with instructors or provide the specialized training themselves.

ASM2009 promoted itself as fostering positive youth development and marketable job skills and thus it must take issues of transfer of learning very seriously and experiment with new methods of working with young people to make successful transfer a reality.

We have much more to say about program implications in the chapters of this book. Readers who went from Chapter 1 directly to this appendix are urged to turn next to those chapters.

---

[61] Durlak et al. (2010).

Appendix 2

Northwestern Mock Job Interview

Barton J. Hirsch, PhD
Northwestern University

Youth Name: _____

Date: _____ Time: _____

Interviewer Name: _____

"Hello, I'm _____ and I'm happy to meet you. During this interview, we'll talk about your application, then I will ask you a number of questions, and finally, I will give you some feedback on how I think the interview went. Does that sound alright with you?"

[Interviewer: read over and discuss the student's job application form.]

"Let me tell you a little about what we're looking for."

[Note: If the position is for a summer internship, you may substitute that term for "job." Be aware, however, that some high school students are not familiar with the concept of an internship.]

Your notes on the youth's response should be written below each question. Ratings should be made after the interview and feedback session is completed and the youth has left the room.

[Note to readers: In the formatting of the actual Northwestern Mock Job Interview, only two interview questions appear on each page. The space between questions was used by interviewers to write notes as the interview proceeded. In the interest of production values, that space has been deleted in this book.]

1A. *What made you decide to apply for this job with us?*

1	2	3	4	5
Was unable to provide a good reason for applying for the job.		Provided one good reason for applying for the job.		Provided three or more good reasons for applying for the job.

2A. *What do you think you could bring to this sort of job; what kinds of experiences have you had in school, an after-school program, a volunteer position, or a part-time job that could apply here?*

1	2	3	4	5
Provided only a general answer and did not relate the experiences to the job described.		Provided at least one specific answer, but did not relate the experiences to the job described.		Provided at least one specific answer and identified two or more ways the experiences could be applied to the job described.

3A. *Can you tell me about a recent goal and what you did to try to achieve it? [if needed, specify that recent = within the past 6–9 months]*

1	2	3	4	5
Provided only a general answer (e.g., I worked it out) that did not identify personal effort or problem solving.		Provided an example that identified one or two specific instances of personal effort or problem solving.		Provided an example that identified two or more instances of intensive personal effort or problem solving.

4A. *This job will involve working together with several other people. Can you tell me about a time you worked with other people in a group or team, and what you did to help the group?*

1	2	3	4	5
Provided only a general answer (e.g. I'm a team player) that did not describe a group experience.		Provided an example but did not identify any effective contributions to the group.		Provided an example and clearly identified one or more effective contributions to the group.

5A. *Can you tell me about a time when you had to complete a project by a deadline, and what you learned from that about how to handle deadlines?*

1	2	3	4	5
Provided only a general answer (e.g., I just got it done).		Provided a specific example, but did not clearly explain what he or she learned from the experience.		Provided a specific example and clearly explained one or more things he or she learned from the experience.

6A. *I'd like you to tell me about a situation in which you had to deal with an angry or unreasonable person. How did you handle the situation; what did you do?*

1	2	3	4	5
Provided only a general answer (e.g., I'm good at keeping my cool) or denied ever being in this situation.		Took some action, but not enough to resolve the situation in a respectful manner.		Took the time to resolve the situation in a respectful manner.

7A. *Let's say you disagree with your boss about the best way to do a job, and you really do not like the method described to you. How would you handle the situation; what would you do?*

1	2	3	4	5
Would do the job, but do it my way.		Would do the job as directed reluctantly, but show frustration and express my opinion about a better method.		Would do the job as directed or express my opinion about a better method in a professional manner.

8A. *This job sometimes requires people to come in to work on short notice or to stay and cover the next shift. How would you handle it if your boss asked you to do this?*

1	2	3	4	5
Probably would not come in or stay late; disliked the idea; mentioned problems or conflicts.		Might come in or stay late if possible; showed reluctance.		Would come in or stay late if possible; no hesitation.

9A. *Say one of your friends has tickets for a special event that you would really enjoy on a day you're scheduled to work. What would you do?*

1	2	3	4	5
Would phone the boss and tell him/her they are sick or give some other reason why they can't come in.		Would phone the boss to see if someone else can cover the shift.		Would go to work on time and decline the friend's invitation; work comes first.

10A. *Imagine that your boss gives you a big photocopying job to do – say thirty copies of a long report for a meeting at noon. When you go to make the copies, the copier breaks down. Your boss has left the office and can't be reached. What would you do?*

1	2	3	4	5
Was unable to describe a strategy.		Described a general strategy (e.g., I would figure it out), or it was unclear how his or her action would resolve the problem.		Described one or more specific strategies (e.g., talk to the secretary; go to Kinko's) that would resolve the problem.

11A. *How do you see this job contributing to your life in the next few years?*

1	2	3	4	5
Was unable to describe a coherent goal or connect the job to any future scenario.		Was able to describe at least one goal, but was not very clear about how the job might connect with the goal.		Was able to describe one or more coherent goals and somehow connected the job to those goals.

12A. *What are some questions you would like to ask me about this job?*

1	2	3	4	5
Did not have any questions to ask, or only asked general questions not related to the job announcement or interview discussion.		Asked one question that was related to the job announcement or interview discussion.		Asked two or more good questions related to the job announcement or the interview discussion.

13A. *What else would you like to tell me about yourself that could help us decide whether you are the right person for this job?*

1	2	3	4	5
The response detracted from my impression of this applicant.		The response neither added to nor detracted from my impression of this applicant.		The response gave me a more positive impression of this applicant.

"Thank you very much for coming in for this interview. I've enjoyed meeting you and learning something about you. I hope this practice job interview was helpful for you. I'd like to give you some feedback about how I think you did in the interview."

Follow-up ratings:

1B. *What was your initial impression of this applicant (e.g., good handshake, appropriate greeting)?*

1	2	3	4	5
The applicant made a poor first impression.		The applicant made a moderately good first impression.		The applicant made an excellent first impression.

2B. *Were the applicant's dress and appearance appropriate for the job interview?*

1	2	3	4	5
The applicant was not dressed neatly for the interview and was not well groomed.		The applicant was adequately dressed for the interview and moderately well groomed.		The applicant was neatly dressed for the interview and very well groomed.

3B. *Did the applicant maintain an appropriate amount of eye contact?*

1	2	3	4	5
The applicant avoided eye contact.		The applicant occasionally made eye contact.		The applicant maintained good eye contact.

4B. *Did the applicant demonstrate a positive attitude toward the job in question?*

1	2	3	4	5
The applicant did not seem interested in or enthusiastic about the job.		The applicant seemed only moderately interested in or enthusiastic about the job.		The applicant seemed very interested in and enthusiastic about the job.

5B. *Did the applicant exhibit positive body language/physical demeanor?*

1	2	3	4	5
The applicant exhibited poor posture, negative expressions, or inappropriate mannerisms throughout the interview.		The applicant occasionally exhibited poor posture, negative expressions, or inappropriate mannerisms.		The applicant exhibited good posture, positive expressions, and no inappropriate mannerisms.

6B. *Did the applicant exhibit an appropriate amount of confidence?*

1	2	3	4	5
The applicant came across as lacking in confidence or displayed considerable defensiveness.		The applicant came across as moderately confident and displayed little defensiveness.		The applicant came across as confident, and displayed no cockiness or defensiveness.

7B. *Did the applicant pay attention?*

1	2	3	4	5
The applicant did not pay attention and was distracted throughout the interview.		The applicant paid some attention during the interview but was occasionally distracted.		The applicant paid close attention throughout the interview without being distracted.

8B. *Did the applicant communicate clearly and persuasively?*

1	2	3	4	5
The applicant did not speak clearly or persuasively.		The applicant spoke with moderate clarity and persuasiveness.		The applicant spoke very clearly and persuasively.

9B. *Is the applicant mature enough for the job?*

1	2	3	4	5
No, this applicant is not sufficiently mature for the job.		The applicant exhibited some evidence of maturity, but I have some concerns.		Yes, this applicant is mature enough for the job.

10B. *How well did the applicant complete the job application?*

1	2	3	4	5
The applicant did a poor job of completing the application.		The applicant did a good job of completing the application.		The applicant did an excellent job of completing the application.

11B. *To what extent have this applicant's prior experiences prepared them for this job?*

1	2	3	4	5
The applicant has almost no experiences that have prepared him for this job.		The applicant has some experiences that have prepared him for this job.		The applicant has many good experiences that have prepared him for this job.

12B. *How did the young person respond to the feedback you provided?*

1	2	3	4	5
The applicant was defensive or seemed upset.		The applicant listened but did not seem to care about my comments		The applicant seemed genuinely interested and appreciated my comments.

13B. *How likely is it that you would hire this applicant for a summer job?*

1	2	3	4	5
I would definitely not hire this applicant.	It is unlikely I would hire this applicant.	I see enough potential in this applicant that I might hire him if I really needed someone. ("Hold Box")	This applicant meets the job criteria and I would be willing to hire him.	I am enthusiastic about this applicant and would definitely hire him.

14B. *How likely is it that you would hire this applicant for a permanent entry-level job?*

1	2	3	4	5
I would definitely not hire this applicant.	It is unlikely I would hire this applicant.	I see enough potential in this applicant that I might hire him if I really needed someone. ("Hold Box")	This applicant meets the job criteria and I would be willing to hire him.	I am enthusiastic about this applicant and would definitely hire him.

For training purposes, a copy of two video interviews, along with consensus ratings by two human resource professionals for each item on the mock job interview (accompanied by the rationale for each rating), is available from either bhirsch@northwestern.edu or rachel.g.hirsch@gmail.com.

REFERENCES

Adelman, H., & Taylor, L. (2003). On sustainability of project innovations as systemic change. *Journal of Educational and Psychological Consultation*, 14, 1–25.

Allensworth, E. (2006). *Update to: From high school to the future: A first look at Chicago Public School graduates' college enrollment college preparation, and graduation from four-year colleges.* Chicago: University of Chicago Consortium on Chicago School Research.

Almlund, M., Duckworth, A., Heckman, J., & Kautz, T. (2011). Personality psychology and economics. In E. Hanushek, S. Machin, & L. Woessmann (Eds.), *Handbook of the economics of education* (Vol. 4, pp. 1–181). Waltham, MA: Elsevier.

Anderson, E. (1999). *Code of the street: Decency, violence, and the moral life of the inner city.* New York: W. W. Norton.

Attle, S., & Baker, B. (2007). Cooperative learning in a competitive environment: Classroom implications. *International Journal of Teaching and Learning in Higher Education*, 19, 77–83.

Bandura, A. (1995). *Self-efficacy in changing societies.* Cambridge: Cambridge University Press.

(1997). *Self-efficacy: The exercise of control.* New York: W. H. Freeman and Company.

Barron, B. J. S. (1998). Doing with understanding: Lessons from research on problem- and project-based learning. *The Journal of the Learning Sciences*, 7, 272–322.

Bartko, W. T., & Eccles, J. S. (2003). Adolescent participation in structured and unstructured activities: A person-oriented analysis. *Journal of Youth and Adolescence*, 32, 233–241.

Baumrind, D. (1966). Effects of authoritative parental control on child behavior. *Child Development*, 37, 887–907.

(1991). Parenting styles and adolescent development. In R. Lerner, A. Petersen, & J. Brooks-Gunn (Eds.), *Encyclopedia of Adolescence* (pp. 746–757). New York: Garland.

(2012). Differentiating between confrontive and coercive kinds of parental power-assertive disciplinary practices. *Human Development*, 55, 35–51.

(2013). Authoritative parenting revisited: History and current status. In R. Larzelere, A. Morris, & A. Harrist (Eds.), *Authoritative parenting: Synthesizing nurturance and discipline for optimal child development* (pp. 11–34). Washington, DC: American Psychological Association.

Bell, D., & Blanchflower, D. (2011). Youth unemployment in Europe and the United States. *Nordic Economic Policy Review, 2,* 11–37.

Benson, P. (1997). *All kids are our kids: What communities must do to raise caring and responsible children and adolescents.* San Francisco: Jossey-Bass.

Berge, J., Wall, M., Loth, K., & Neumark-Sztainer, D. (2010). Parenting style as a predictor of adolescent weight and weight-related behaviors. *Journal of Adolescent Health, 46,* 331–338.

Berger, S., & Piore, M. (1980). *Dualism and discontinuity in industrial societies.* Cambridge: Cambridge University Press.

Berman, P., & McLaughlin, M. (1978). *Federal programs supporting educational change, Vol. 8: Implementing and sustaining innovations.* Washington, DC: U.S. Office of Education.

Berry, C., Sackett, P., & Landers, R. (2007). Revisiting interview-cognitive ability relationships: Attending to specific range restriction mechanisms in meta-analysis. *Personnel Psychology, 60,* 837–874.

Betsey, C., Hollister, R., & Papageorgiou, M. (1985) (Eds.). *Youth employment and training programs: The YEPDA years.* Washington, DC: National Academies Press.

Bouffard, S. M., Wimer, C., Caronongan, P., Little, P. M. D., Dearing, E., & Simpkins, S. D. (2006). Demographic differences in patterns of youth out-of-school time activity participation. *Journal of Youth Development, 1*(1).

Bowles, S., & Gintis, H. (1976). *Schooling in capitalist America: Educational reform and the contradictions of economic life.* New York: Basic Books.

Bowles, S., Gintis, H., & Osbourne, M. (2001). The determinants of earnings: Skills, preferences, and schooling. *Journal of Economic Literature, 39,* 1137–1176.

Bronfenbrenner, U. (1979). *The ecology of human development.* Cambridge, MA: Harvard University Press.

Brown, B., & Larson, J. (2009). Peer relationships in adolescence. In R. Lerner & L. Steinberg (Eds.), *Handbook of adolescent psychology (3rd ed., Vol. 2): Contextual influences on adolescent development* (pp. 74–103). Hoboken, NJ: John Wiley & Sons.

Browne, A. L., & Campione, J. C. (1996). Psychological theory and the design of innovative learning environments: On procedures, principles, and systems. In L. Schauble & R. Glasner (Eds.), *Innovations in learning: New environments for education* (pp. 289–325). Mahwah, NJ: Lawrence Erlbaum.

Cahuc, P., Carcillo, S., & Zimmerman, K. (2013). *The employment of the low-skilled youth in France.* IZA Policy Paper #64. Bonn, Germany: Institute for the Study of Labor (IZA).

Carnegie Corporation of New York. (1992). *A matter of time: Risk and opportunity in the nonschool hours.* New York: Author.

Carr, R., Wright, J., & Brody, C. (1996). Effects of high school work experience a decade later: Evidence from the National Longitudinal Survey. *Sociology of Education, 69,* 66–81.

Casner-Lotto, J., & Barrington, L. (2006). *Are they really ready to work? Employers' perspectives on the basic knowledge and applied skills of new entrants to the 21st century US workforce.* Washington, DC: Conference Board, Partnership for 21st Century Skills, Corporate Voices for Working Families, & Society for Human Resource Management.

Castrucci, B., & Gerlach, K. (2006). Understanding the association between authoritative parenting and smoking. *Maternal and Child Health Journal,* 10, 217–224.

Chaiken, M. (1998). Tailoring established after-school programs to meet urban realities. In D. Elliott, B. Hamburg, & K. Williams (Eds.), *Violence in American schools: A new perspective* (pp. 348–375). New York: Cambridge University Press.

Cheney, L. (1998). Limited horizons. *The New York Times,* February 3.

Connell, J., Gambone, M., & Smith, T. (2000). *Youth development in community settings: Challenges to our field and our approach.* Philadelphia: Public/Private Ventures.

Conrad, C. A. (1999). *Soft skills and the minority work force.* Washington, DC: Joint Center for Political and Economic Studies.

Corno, L. (1993). The best laid plans: Modern conceptions of volition and educational research. *Educational Researcher,* 22, 13–22.

Cotterell, J. L. (1996). *Social networks and social influences in adolescence.* New York: Routledge.

Csikszentmihalyi, M., & Schneider, B. (2000). *Becoming adult: How teenagers prepare for the world of work.* New York: Basic Books.

Currie, J., & Thomas, D. (1999). Early test scores, socioeconomic status and future outcomes. *National Bureau of Economic Research.* Retrieved from http://www.nber.org/papers/w6943

Darling, N. (1999). Parenting style and its correlates. ERIC Digest. Retrieved from http://csped.com/educator/earlychildhood/articles/parentingstyle.pdf

DeCoursey, J., & Skyles, A. (2007). *Making connections: Engaging employers in preparing Chicago's youth for the workforce.* Chicago: Chapin Hall, University of Chicago.

DeGroot, T., & Motowidlo, S. J. (1999). Why visual and vocal interview cues can affect interviewers' judgments and predict job performance. *Journal of Applied Psychology,* 84, 986–993.

Deutsch, N. L. (2008). *Pride in the projects: Teens building identities in urban contexts.* New York: NYU Press.

Dever, B., & Karabenick, S. (2011). Is authoritative teaching beneficial for all students? A multi-level model of the effects of teaching style on interest and achievement. *School Psychology Quarterly,* 26, 131–144.

Dipboye, R., Macan, T., & Shahani-Denning, C. (2012). The selection interview from the interviewer and applicant perspectives: Can't have one without the other. In N. Schmitt (Ed.), *The Oxford handbook of personnel assessment and selection* (pp. 323–352). New York: Oxford University Press.

Doeringer, P., & Piore, M. (1971). *Internal labor markets and manpower analysis.* Lexington, MA: Heath Lexington Books.

Douglas, P. (1921). American apprenticeship and industrial education. *Studies in History, Economics and Public Law,* 95, 209–550.

DuBois, D., & Karcher, M. (Eds.). (2014). *Handbook of youth mentoring* (2nd ed.). Thousand Oaks, CA: SAGE.

Duckworth, K., Duncan, G., Kokko, K., Lyrra, A, Metzger, M., & Simonton, S. (2014). *The relative importance of adolescent skills and behaviors for adult earnings: A cross-national study.* Irvine, CA: UCI Network on Interventions in Development.

Durlak, J. (1998). Why program implementation is important. *Journal of Prevention & Intervention in the Community, 17,* 5–18.

Durlak, J., & Dupre, E. (2008). Implementation matters: A review of research on the influence of implementation on program outcomes and the factors affecting implementation. *American Journal of Community Psychology, 41,* 327–350.

Durlak, J. A., Weissberg, R. P., & Pachan, M. (2010). A meta-analysis of after-school programs that seek to promote personal and social skills in children and adolescents. *American Journal of Community Psychology, 46,* 294–309.

Eccles, J. S., & Gootman, J. A. (Eds.). (2002). *Community programs to promote youth development.* Washington, DC: National Academies Press.

Edelman, P., Holzer, H., & Offner, P. (2006). *Reconnecting disadvantaged young men.* Washington, DC: Urban Institute Press.

Edelson, D. C. (2001). Learning-for-use: A framework for the design of technology-supported inquiry activities. *Journal of Research in Science Teaching, 28,* 355–385.

Eder, R., & Harris, M. (Eds.) (1999). *The employment interview handbook.* Thousand Oaks, CA: SAGE.

Elias, M. (1997). Reinterpreting dissemination of prevention programs as widespread implementation with effectiveness and fidelity. In R. Weissberg, T. Gullotta, R. Hampton, B. Ryan, et al. (Eds.), *Healthy children 2010: Establishing preventive services* (pp. 253–289). Thousand Oaks, CA: SAGE.

Ellwood, D. (1980). Teenage unemployment: Permanent scars or temporary blemishes? In R. Freeman & D. Wise (Eds.), *The youth labor market problem: Its natures, causes, and consequences* (pp. 349–390). Chicago: University of Chicago Press.

Elmore, R. (1979/1980). Backward mapping: Implementation research and policy decisions. *Political Science Quarterly, 94,* 601–616.

(1985). Forward and backward mapping: Reversible logic in the analysis of public policy. In K. Hanf & T. Toonen (Eds.), *Policy implementation in federal and unitary systems: Questions of analysis and design* (pp. 33–70). Boston: Martinus Nijhoff.

Emmenegger, P., Hausermann, S., Palier, B., & Seeleib-Kaiser, M. (Eds.) (2012). *The age of dualization: The changing face of inequality in deindustrializing societies.* Oxford: Oxford University Press.

Ensminger, M. E., Forrest, C. B., Riley, A. W., Kang, M. S., Green, B. F., Starfield, B., & Ryan, S. A. (2000). The validity of measures of socioeconomic status of adolescents. *Journal of Adolescent Research, 15,* 392–419.

Entwisle, D., Alexander, K., & Olson, L. (2000). Early work histories of urban youth. *American Sociological Review, 65,* 279–297.

Erikson, E. (1968). *Identity: Youth and crisis.* New York: W. W. Norton.

European Commission (2013). *Working together for Europe's young people: A call to action on youth unemployment.* Brussels: Author.

Ewing, J., & Eddy, M. (2013). European leaders grapple with youth unemployment. *The New York Times,* May 14, 2013.

Feldman, A. F., & Matjasko, J. L. (2005). The role of school-based extracurricular activities in adolescent development: A comprehensive review and future directions. *Review of Educational Research,* 75, 159–210.

(2007). Profiles and portfolios of adolescent school-based extracurricular activity participation. *Journal of Adolescence,* 30, 313–332.

Fixsen, D., Naoom, S., Blasé, K., & Friedman, R. (2005). *Implementation research: A synthesis of the literature.* Tampa, FL: Florida Mental Health Institute, University of South Florida.

Flores-Gonzalez, N. (2002). *School kids/street kids: Identity development in Latino students.* New York: Teachers College Press.

(2005). Popularity versus respect: School structure, peer groups and Latino academic achievement. *International Journal of Qualitative Studies in Education,* 18, 625–642.

Freeman, R., & Holzer, H. (1986) (Eds.) *The black youth employment crisis.* Chicago: University of Chicago Press.

Gee, J. (1996). *Social linguistics and literacies: Ideology in discourses* (2nd ed.). New York: Teachers College Press.

Gestsdottir, S., & Lerner, R. (2008). Positive development in adolescence: The development and role of intentional self-regulation. *Human Development,* 51, 202–224.

Goerge, R., Chaskin, R., & Guiltinan, S. (2006). *What high school students in the Chicago Public Schools do in their out-of-school time: 2003–2005.* Chicago: Chapin Hall, University of Chicago.

Goerge, R., Cusick, G., Wasserman, M., & Gladden, R. (2007). *After-school programs and academic impact: A study of Chicago's After School Matters.* Chicago: Chapin Hall, University of Chicago.

Gottfredson, D. C., Cross, A. B., Wilson, D., Rorie, M., & Connell, N. (2010). Effects of participation in after-school programs for middle school students: A randomized trial. *Journal of Research on Educational Effectiveness,* 3, 282–313.

Gottfredson, D., Fink, C., Skroban, S., & Gottfredson, G. (1997). Making prevention work. In R. Weissberg, T. Gullotta, R. Hampton, B. Ryan, et al. (Eds), *Healthy children 2010: Establishing preventive services* (pp. 219–252). Thousand Oaks, CA: SAGE.

Gottfredson, D. C., Gerstenblith, S. A., Soule, D. A., Womer, S. C., & Lu, S. (2004). Do after school programs reduce delinquency? *Prevention Science,* 5, 253–266.

Gottfredson, D., Gottfredson, G., & Skroban, S. (1998). Can prevention work where it is needed most? *Evaluation Review,* 22, 315–340.

Greenberger, E., & Steinberg, L. (1986). *When teenagers work: The psychological and social costs of adolescent employment.* New York: Basic Books.

Gregg, P., & Tominey, E. (2005). The wage scar from male youth unemployment. *Labour Economics,* 12, 487–509.

Gregory, A., & Weinstein, R. (2004). Connection and regulation at home and in school predicting growth in achievement for adolescents. *Journal of Adolescent Research*, 19, 405–427.

Hahn, A., Leavitt, T., & Aaron, P. (1994). *Evaluation of the Quantum Opportunities Program demonstration: Short-term impacts*. Washington, DC: Mathematica Policy Research.

Halpern, R. (2003). *Making play work: The promise of after-school programs for low-income children*. New York: Teachers College Press.

   (2006). After-School Matters in Chicago: Apprenticeship as a model for youth programming. *Youth & Society*, 38, 203–235.

   (2009). *The means to grow up: Reinventing apprenticeship as a developmental support in adolescence*. New York: Routledge.

Halpern, R. with F. Kimondo (2005, January). *A qualitative study of After School Matters (interim report)*. Chicago, IL: Erikson Institute.

Hamilton, S. F. (1990). *Apprenticeship for adulthood: Preparing youth for the future*. New York: Free Press.

Hamilton, S. F., & Hamilton, M. A. (2004). Contexts for mentoring: Adolescent-adult relationships in workplaces and communities. In R. Lerner & L. Steinberg (Eds.), *Handbook of adolescent psychology* (pp. 395–428). Hoboken, NJ: John Wiley & Sons.

Hansen, D. M., & Larson, R. (2002). *The Youth Experience Survey*. Unpublished manuscript, University of Illinois at Urbana–Champaign.

Hansen, D. M., Larson, R. W., & Dworkin, J. B. (2003). What adolescents learn in organized youth activities: A survey of self-reported developmental experiences. *Journal of Research on Adolescence*, 13, 25–55.

Harhoff, D., & Kane, T. (1997). Is the German apprenticeship system a panacea for the U. S. labor market? *Journal of Population Economics*, 10, 171–196.

Hawkins, J. D., Catalano, R., & Associates. (1992). *Communities that care: Action for drug abuse*. San Francisco: Jossey-Bass.

Healey, K., Nagaoka, J., & Michelman, V. (2014). *The educational attainment of Chicago Public School students: A focus on four-year college degrees*. Chicago: University of Chicago Consortium on Chicago School Research.

Heckman, J., & Rubinstein, Y. (2001). The importance of noncognitive skills: Lessons from GET testing program. *American Economic Review*, 91, 145–149.

Heckman, J., Stixrud, J., & Urzua, S. (2006). The effects of cognitive and noncognitive abilities on labor market outcomes and social behavior. *Journal of Labor Economics*, 24, 411–482.

Heifetz, R. (1994). *Leadership without easy answers*. Cambridge, MA: Harvard University Press.

Hershey, A. (2003). Has school-to-work worked? In Stull, W. & Sanders, N. (Eds.), *The school-to-work movement: Origins and destinations* (pp. 79–100). Westport, CT: Praeger.

Hirsch, B. J. (2005). *A place to call home: After-school programs for urban youth*. Washington, DC: American Psychological Association and New York: Teachers College Press.

Hirsch, B. J., Deutsch, N. L., & DuBois, D. L. (2011). *After-school programs and youth development: Case studies of success and failure*. New York: Cambridge University Press.

Hirsch, B. J., Hedges, L. V., Stawicki, J., & Mekinda, M. A. (2011). *After-School Programs for high school students: An evaluation of After School Matters.* Technical Report. New York: Wallace Foundation.

Hirsch, B. J., & Riger, S. (1989). Summer job programs in the private sector for Chicago youth. Paper presented at the Center for Urban Affairs and Policy Research, Northwestern University (May).

Holzer, H. (1996). *What employers want: Job prospects for less-educated workers.* New York: Russell Sage.

Huffcutt, A. I. (2011). An empirical review of the employment interview construct literature. *International Journal of Selection and Assessment*, 19, 62–81.

Huffcutt, A. I., Conway, J. M., Roth, P. L., & Stone, N. J. (2001). Identification and meta-analytic assessment of psychological constructs measured in employment interviews. *Journal of Applied Psychology*, 86, 897–913.

Huffcutt, A. I., & Roth, P. L. (1998). Racial group differences in employment interview evaluations. *Journal of Applied Psychology*, 83, 179–189.

Huffcutt, A. I., Van Iddenkinge, C. H., & Roth, P. L. (2011). Understanding applicant behavior in employment interviews: A theoretical model of interviewee performance. *Human Resource Management Review*, 21, 353–367.

Hughes, J. (2002). Authoritative teaching: Tipping the balance in favor of school versus peer effects. *Journal of School Psychology*, 40, 485–492.

Hynes, K., & Hirsch, B. J. (Eds.) (2012). Career programming: Linking youth to the world of work. *New Directions in Youth Development*, 134, 1–117.

Jackson, S. L., Krajcik, J., & Soloway, E. (1998). The design of guided learner-adaptable scaffolding in interactive learning environments. Proceedings of ACM CHI'98, pp. 187–194. ACM Press.

James-Burdumy, S., Dynarski, M., & Deke, J. (2008). After-school program effects on behavior: Results from the 21st Century Community Learning Centers Program national evaluation. *Economic Inquiry*, 46, 13–18.

Johnson, D., & Johnson, R. (1989). *Cooperation and competition: Theory and research.* Edina, MN: Interaction Book Company,

 (1999). *Learning together and alone: Cooperative, competitive, and individualistic learning* (5th ed.). Boston: Allyn & Bacon.

 (2005). New developments in social interdependency theory. *Genetic, Social, and General Psychology Monographs*, 131, 285–358.

Karoly, P. (1993). Mechanisms of self-regulation: A system view. *Annual Review of Psychology*, 44, 23–52.

Kazis, R., & Pennington, H. (2003). What's next for school-to-career? An assessment of progress and prospects. In Stull, W., & Sanders, N. (Eds.), *The school-to-work movement: Origins and destinations* (pp. 263–283). Westport, CT: Praeger.

Kelly, B., & Perkins, D. (Eds.) (2012). *Handbook of implementation science for psychology in education.* New York: Cambridge University Press.

Kemple, J. (2008). *Career academies: Long-term impacts on labor market outcomes, educational attainment, and transition to adulthood.* New York: MDRC.

Kemple, J., & Snipes, J. (2000). *Career academies: Impacts on students' engagement and performance in high school.* New York: MDRC.

Kett, J. (1977). *Rites of passage: Adolescence in America, 1790 to the present.* New York: Basic Books.

Kirk, R. (1995). *Experimental design*. Belmont, CA: Brooks Cole.

Kohn, A. (1992). *No contest: The case against competition*. New York: Houghton Mifflin Harcourt.

Kuhn, P., & Weinberger, C. (2005). Leadership skills and wages. *Journal of Labor Economics*, 23, 395–436,

Larson R. W. (2000). Toward a psychology of positive youth development. *American Psychologist*, 55, 170–183.

Larson, R. W. (2007). From "I" to 'We": Development of the capacity for teamwork in youth programs. In R. Silbereisen & R. Lerner (Eds.), *Approaches to positive youth development* (pp. 277–292). Thousand Oaks, CA: SAGE.

Larson, R. W., & Angus, R. (2011). Adolescents' development of skills for agency in youth programs: Learning to think strategically. *Child Development*, 82, 277–294.

Larzelere, R., Morris, A., & Harrist, A. (Eds.) (2012). *Authoritative parenting: Synthesizing nurturance and discipline for optimal child development*. Washington, DC: American Psychological Association.

Lauer, P. Akiba, M., Wilkerson, S., Apthorp, H., Snow, D., & Martin-Glenn, M. (2006). Out-of-school time programs: A meta-analysis of effects for at-risk students. *Review of Educational Research*, 76, 275–313.

Lazear, E. P. (2003). Teacher incentives. *Swedish Economic Policy Review*. 10, 179–214.

Lerman, R. (2003). Is the school-to-work movement on the right track? In Stull, W. & Sanders, N. (Eds.), *The school-to-work movement: Origins and destinations* (pp. 221–238). Westport, CT: Praeger.

(2013). Are employability skills learned in U.S. youth education and training programs? *IZA Journal of Labor Policy*, 2, 6.

Lerner, R. M. (2004). *Liberty: Thriving and civic engagement among America's youth*. Thousand Oaks, CA: SAGE.

Levashina, J., Hartwell, C., Morgeson, F., & Campion, M. (2014). The structured employment interview: Narrative and quantitative review of the research literature. *Personnel Psychology*, 67, 241–293.

Lievens, F., Highhouse, S., & De Corte, W. (2005). The importance of traits and abilities in supervisors' hirability decisions as a function of method of assessment. *Journal of Occupational and Organizational Psychology*, 78, 453–470.

Lindqvist, E., & Vestman, R. (2011). The labor market returns to cognitive and non-cognitive ability: Evidence from the Swedish enlistment. *American Economic Journal: Applied Economics*, 3, 101–128.

Luszczynska, A., Diehl, M., Gutierrez-Dona, B., Kuusinen, P., & Schwarzer, R. (2004). Measuring one component of dispositional self-regulation: Attention control in goal pursuit. *Personality and Individual Differences*, 37, 555–566.

Macan, T. (2009). The employment interview: A review of current studies and directions for future research. *Human Resource Management Review*, 19, 203–218.

Maccoby, E., & Martin, J. (1983). Socialization in the context of the family: Parent-child interaction. In P. Mussen (Ed.), *Handbook of child psychology* (4th ed., Vol. 4, pp. 1–101). New York: John Wiley & Sons.

Mahoney, J. L., Larson, R. W., & Eccles, J. S. (2005). *Organized activities as contexts of development: Extracurricular activities, after-school, and community programs*. Mahwah, NJ: Lawrence Erlbaum.

Mahoney, J. L., Vandell, D. L., Simpkins, S., & Zarrett, N. (2009). Adolescent out-of-school activities. In R. M. Lerner & L. Steinberg (Eds.), *Handbook of adolescent psychology* (3rd ed. Vol. 2): *Contextual influences on adolescent development* (pp. 228–269). Hoboken, NJ: John Wiley & Sons.

Mandara, J. (2006). How family functioning influences African American males' academic achievement: A review and clarification of the empirical literature. *Teachers College Record*, 10, 205–222.

Masten, A., Desjardins, C., McCormick, C., Kuo, S., & Long, S. (2010). The significance of childhood competence and problems for adult success at work: A developmental cascade analysis. *Development and Psychopathology*, 22, 679–694.

Maurer, T., & Solaman, J. (2006). The science and practice of a structured interview coaching program. *Personnel Psychology*, 59, 433–456.

Maxfield, M., Schirm, A., & Rodriguez-Planas, N. (2003). *The Quantum Opportunities Program demonstration: Implementation and short-term impacts*. Washington, DC: Mathematica Policy Research.

McLaughlin, M., Irby, M., & Langman, J. (1994). *Urban sanctuaries: Neighborhood organizations in the lives and futures of innter-city youth*. San Francisco: Jossey-Bass.

McNeal, R. B. (1998). High school extracurricular activities: Closed structures and stratifying patterns of participation. *The Journal of Educational Research*, 91, 183–191.

Mekinda, M. (2014). Support for career development in youth: Program models and evaluation. *New Directions in Youth Development*, 134, 45–54.

(2015). *After-school programs and support for work readiness: A qualitative evaluation of After School Matters*. Unpublished dissertation, Northwestern University, Evanston.

Mekinda, M., & Hirsch, B. (2010). *Quality of work vs. non-work after-school activities for low-income, minority youth*. Unpublished manuscript, Northwestern University.

Moos, R. H. (1974). *The social climate scales: An overview*. Palo Alto, CA: Consulting Psychologists Press.

Mortimer, J. (2003). *Working and growing up in America*. Cambridge, MA: Harvard University Press.

Mortimer, J., & Kruger, H. (2006). Pathways from school to work in Germany and the United States. In M. Hallinan (Ed.), *Handbook of the sociology of education* (pp. 475–497). New York: Kluwer Academic/Plenum Press.

Mortimer, J., Pimentel, E., Rye, S., Nash, K., & Lee, C. (1996). Part-time work and occupational value formation in adolescence. *Social Forces*, 74, 1305–1318.

Moss, P. I., & Tilly, C. (1996). "Soft" skills and race. *Work and Occupations*, 23, 252–276.

(2001). *Stories employers tell: Race, skill, and hiring in America*. New York: Russell Sage.

Mroz, T., & Savage, T. (2006). The long-term effects of youth unemployment. *Journal of Human Resources*, 41, 259–293.

Mulligan, C. B. (1999). Galton versus the human capital approach to inheritance. *Journal of Political Economy*, 107, 184–224.

Munoz, M. (2005). Backward mapping. In S. Mathison (Ed.), *Encyclopedia of evaluation* (pp. 30–31). Thousand Oaks, CA: SAGE.

Murnane, R. J., & Levy, F. (1996). *Teaching the new basic skills: Principles for educating children to thrive in a changing economy*. New York: Free Press.

Murnane, R. J., Willett, J. B., Duhaldeborde, Y., & Tyler, J. (2000). How important are the cognitive skills of teenagers in predicting subsequent earnings? *Journal of Policy Analysis and Management*, 19, 547–568.

National Research Council. (2012). *Education for life and work: Developing transferable knowledge and skills in the 21st century* (J. Pellegrino & M. Hilton, Eds.). Washington, DC: National Academies Press.

National Research Council and Institute of Medicine. (2002). *Community programs to promote youth development* (J. Eccles & J. Gootman, Eds.). Washington, DC: National Academies Press.

National Research Council and Institute of Medicine, Committee on Increasing High School Students' Engagement and Motivation to Learn. (2003). *Engaging schools: Fostering high school students' motivation to learn*. Washington, DC: National Academies Press.

National Research Council and Institute of Medicine. (2005). *Growing up global: The changing transitions to adulthood in developing countries*. Washington, DC: National Academies Press.

Neckerman, K. (2007). *Schools betrayed: Roots of failure in inner-city education*. Chicago: University of Chicago Press.

Neckerman, K., & Kirschenman, J. (1991). Hiring strategies, racial bias, and inner city workers. *Social Problems*, 38, 433–447.

Neumark, D. (Ed.) (2007). *Improving school-to-work transitions*. New York: Russell Sage.

Newman, K. (1999). *No shame in my game: The working poor in the inner city*. New York: Vintage Books and Russell Sage.

Noam, G., Biancarosa, G., & Dechausay, N. (2003). *Afterschool education: Approaches to an emerging field*. Cambridge, MA: Harvard Education Press.

Organisation for Economic Co-operation and Development (OECD). (2010). *Off to a good start? Jobs for youth*. Paris: OECD Publishing.

Owens, A., & Schneider, B. (2005). Self-regulation and the transition to adulthood. *Academic Exchange Quarterly*, 9, 62–67.

Partnership for 21st Century Skills. (2008). *Transition brief: Policy recommendations on preparing Americans for the global skills race*. Tuscon, AZ: Partnership for 21st Century Skills.

Pedersen, S., & Seidman, E. (2005). Contexts and correlates of out-of-school activity participation among low-income urban adolescents. In J. L. Mahoney, R. W. Larson & J. S. Eccles (Eds.), *Organized activities as contexts of development: Extracurricular activities, after-school and community programs* (pp. 85–109). Mahwah, NJ: Lawrence Erlbaum.

Perkins, D. N., & Salomon, G. (1992). Transfer of learning. *International Encyclopedia of Education, 2*. Retrieved from http://learnweb.harvard.edu/alps/thinking/docs/traencyn.htm

Pittman, K., Irby, M., & Ferber, T. (2000). *Unfinished business: Further reflections on a decade of promoting youth development*. Philadelphia: Public/Private Ventures.

Quinn, J. (1999). Where need meets opportunity: Youth development programs for early teens. *The Future of Children*, 9, 96–116.

Quiroz, P., Gonzalez, N., & Frank, K. (1996). Carving a niche in the high school social structure: Formal and informal constraints on participation in the extra curriculum. *Research in Sociology of Education and Socialization*, 11, 93–120.

Raudenbush, S. W., & Bryk, A. S. (2002). *Hierarchical linear models*. Thousand Oaks, CA: SAGE.

Reeve, J., & Deci, E. (1996). Elements of the competitive situation that affect intrinsic motivation. *Personality and Social Psychology Bulletin*, 22, 24–33.

Rhodes, J. (2002). *Stand by me: The risks and rewards of mentoring today's youth*. Cambridge, MA: Harvard University Press.

Roberts, B. W., Kuncel, N. R., Shiner, R., Caspi, A., & Goldberg, L. R. (2007). The power of personality: The comparative validity of personality traits, socioeconomic status, and cognitive ability for predicting important life outcomes. *Perspectives on Psychological Science*, 2, 313–345.

Roderick, M., Nagaoka, J., & Allensworth, E. (2006). *From high school to the future: A first look at Chicago Public School graduates' college enrollment, college preparation, and graduation from four-year colleges*. Chicago: University of Chicago Consortium on Chicago School Research.

Rogoff, B. (1990). *Apprenticeship in thinking: Cognitive development in social context*. New York: Oxford University Press.

(2003). *The cultural nature of human development*. New York: Oxford University Press.

Rose, H. (2006). Do gains in test scores explain labor market outcomes? *Economics of Education Review*, 25, 430–446.

Rosenbaum, J. (2001). *Beyond college for all: Career paths for the forgotten half*. New York: Russell Sage.

(2003). High schools' role in college and workforce preparation: Do college-for-all policies make high school irrelevant? In Stull, W., & Sanders, N. (Eds.), *The school-to-work movement: Origins and destinations* (pp. 203–217). Westport, CT: Praeger.

Roth, P. L., BeVier, C. A., Switzer III, F. S., & Schippmann, J. S. (1996). Meta-analyzing the relationship between grades and job performance. *Journal of Applied Psychology*, 81, 548–556.

Ruhm, C. (1997). Is high school employment consumption or investment? *Journal of Labor Economics*, 15, 735–776.

Rumberger, R., & Larson, K. (1998). Student mobility and the increased risk of high school dropout. *American Journal of Education*, 107, 1–35.

Ryan, P. (2001). The school-to-work transition: A cross-national perspective. *Journal of Economic Literature*, 39, 34–92.

Salomon, G., & Perkins, D. N. (1989). Rocky roads to transfer: Rethinking mechanism of a neglected phenomenon. *Educational Psychologist*, 24, 113–142.

Scarlett, W., Ponte, I., & Singh, J. (2009). *Approaches to behavior and classroom management: Integrating discipline and care*. Thousand Oaks, CA: SAGE.

Schank, R. C. (1995). *Dynamic memory revisited*. New York: Cambridge University Press.

Schoon, I., & Silbereisen, R. (Eds.) (2009). *Transitions from school to work: Globalization, individualization, and patterns of diversity.* New York: Cambridge University Press.

Schorr, L. (1989). *Within our reach.* New York: Doubleday.

Schug, M., & Western, R. (2003). School-to-work: The Wisconsin experience. In W. Stull & N. Sanders (Eds.), *The school-to-work movement: Origins and destinations* (pp. 113–134). Westport, CT: Praeger.

Secretary's Commission on Achieving Necessary Skills (SCANS). (1991a). *What work requires of schools.* Washington, DC: U.S. Department of Labor.

Secretary's Commission on Achieving Necessary Skills (SCANS). (1991b). *Skills and tasks for jobs: A SCANS report for America 2000.* Washington, DC: U.S. Department of Labor.

Sherer, M., Maddux, J., Mercandante, B., Prentice-Dunn, S., Jacobs, B., & Rogers, R. (1982). The self-efficacy scale: Construction and validation. *Psychological Reports, 51,* 663–671.

Snyder, H., & Sickmund, M. (1999). *Juvenile offenders and victims: 1999 National Report.* Washington, DC: Office of Juvenile Justice and Delinquency Prevention.

Spillane, J. P. (2006). *Distributed leadership.* San Francisco: Jossey-Bass.

Staff, J., Messersmith E., & Schulenberg, J. (2009). Adolescents and the world of work. In R. Lerner & L. Steinberg (Eds.), *Handbook of adolescent psychology* (3rd ed., Vol. 2, pp. 270–313). Hoboken, NJ: John Wiley & Sons.

Stanne, M., Johnson, D., & Johnson, R. (1999). Does competition enhance or inhibit motor performance: A meta-analysis. *Psychological Bulletin, 125,* 133–154.

Steadman, H. (2010). *The state of apprenticeship in 2010: International comparisons: Australia, Austria, England, Germany, Ireland, Sweden, Switzerland.* London: London School of Economics and Political Science, Centre for Economic Performance.

Steinberg, L. (2001). We know some things: Parent-adolescent relationships in retrospect and prospect. *Journal of Research on Adolescence, 11,* 1–19.

Steinberg, L., Elmen, J., & Mounts N. (1989). Authoritative parenting, psychosocial maturity, and academic success among adolescents. *Child Development, 60,* 1424–1436.

Stern, D. (2003). Career academies and high-school reform before, during, and after the school-work movement. In W. Stull & N. Sanders (Eds.), *The school-to-work movement: Origins and destinations* (pp. 239–262). Westport, CT: Praeger.

Stone III, J. R., & Lewis, M. V. (2012). *College and career ready in the 21st century: Making high school matter.* New York: Teachers College Press.

Strauss, A., & Corbin, J. (1994). Grounded Theory Methodology – An Overview. In N. K. Denzin & Y. S. Lincoln (Eds.), *Handbook of qualitative research* (pp. 273–285). Thousand Oaks CA: SAGE.

Stull, W. (2003). School-to-work in schools: An overview. In W. Stull, & N. Sanders(Eds.), *The school-to-work movement: Origins and destinations* (pp. 3–26). Westport, CT: Praeger.

Stull, W., & Sanders, N. (Eds.) (2003). *The school-to-work movement: Origins and destinations.* Westport, CT: Praeger.

Symonds, W., Schwartz, R., & Ferguson, R. (2011). *Pathways to prosperity: Meeting the challenge of preparing young Americans for the 21st century*. Cambridge, MA: Harvard University, Graduate School of Education.

Tauer, J., & Harackiewicz, J. (1999). Winning isn't everything: Competition, achievement orientation, and intrinsic motivation. *Journal of Experimental Social Psychology*, 35, 209–238.

(2004). The effects of cooperation and competition on intrinsic motivation and performance. *Interpersonal Relations and Group Processes*, 86, 849–861.

Thompson, D. (2013). Europe's record youth unemployment: The scariest graph in the world just got scarier. *The Atlantic*, May 31, 2013.

Tienda, M., & Ahituv, A. (1996). Ethnic differences in school departure: Does youth employment promote or undermine educational attainment? In G. Mangum & S. Mangum (Eds.), *Of heart and mind: Social policy essays in honor of Sar Levitan* (pp. 93–110). Kalamazoo, MI: Upjohn Institute.

Topor, D., Colarelli, S., & Han, K. (2007). Influences of traits and assessment methods on human resource practitioners' evaluation of job applicants. *Journal of Business and Psychology*, 21, 361–376.

Undry, J. R. (1998). *The National Longitudinal Study of Adolescent Health (ADD HEALTH), waves I & II, 1994–1996: A user's guide*. Los Altos, CA: Sociometrics Corporation.

Voelkl, K. E. (1996). Measuring students' identification with school. *Educational and Psychological Measurement*, 56, 760–770.

Vygotsky, L. S. (1978). *Mind in society: The development of higher psychological processes*. Cambridge, MA: Harvard University Press.

Waddell, G. (2006). Labor-Market consequences of poor attitude and low self-esteem in youth. *Economic Inquiry*, 44, 69–97.

Walker, J. (2008). Looking at teacher practices through the lens of parenting style. *Journal of Experimental Education*, 76, 218–240.

Wentzel, K. (2002). Are effective teachers like good parents? Teaching styles and student adjustment in early adolescence. *Child Development*, 73, 287–301.

Whalen, S. P., DeCoursey, J., & Skyles, A. (2003). *Preparing youth for the workforce: Exploring employer engagement in the Chicago region*. Chicago: Chapin Hall, University of Chicago.

Wilson, J. (2012). *The truly disadvantaged: The inner city the underclass, and public policy* (2nd ed.). Chicago: University of Chicago Press.

Wood, R., & Bandura, A. (1989). Impact of conceptions of ability on self-regulatory mechanisms and complex decision making. *Journal of Personal and Social Psychology*, 56, 407–415.

Wynne, E. (1995). Cooperation-competition: An instructional strategy. *Phi Delta Kappan*, 387, 7–27.

Zemsky, R. (2003). A melding of international perspectives. In W. Stull & N. Sanders (Eds.), *The school-to-work movement: Origins and destinations* (pp. 135–148). Westport, CT: Praeger.

Zief, S., Lauver, S., & Maynard, R. (2006). Impacts of after-school programs on student outcomes. *Campbell Systematic Reviews*, 3, 1–52.

Zimmerman, B. (1995a). Self-regulation involves more than metacognition: A social cognitive perspective. *Educational Psychologist*, 30, 217–221.

(1995b). Self-efficacy and educational development. In A. Bandura (Ed.), *Self-efficacy in changing societies* (pp. 202–231). Cambridge: Cambridge University Press.

(1990). Self-regulating academic learning and achievement: The emergence of a social cognitive perspective. *Educational Psychology Review*, 2, 173–201.

INDEX

CPSIA information can be obtained at www.ICGtesting.com
Printed in the USA
LVOW11s0803200316

479906LV00001B/20/P